Lean and Green Cookbook 2021

Lean and Green Recipes & Fueling Recipes to Make Your Weight Loss Easier and Healthier.

Sandra Brockington

Table of Contents

Chapter 15. Desserts 82

Conclusion 91

Introduction

The Lean and Green diet is not meant for a specific community but aims to cater to individuals who choose to avoid "overanalyzing" an eating schedule. Five out of the six small meals a day are pre-planned and pre-packaged with Lean and Green 's famous '5 & 1' plan, removing the need for any major choices when it's time to feed. Lean and Green happens to be a choice of individuals with a packed schedule, but the reduced-calorie strategy of the product is meant for anybody who wishes to lose weight. As a diet product, a strict lifestyle is expected on the part of the consumer who wishes to follow the diet.

The Lean and Green diet is the brainchild of one Rohan Patel, who in 2008 had suffered from a heart attack. Patel was advised to consume foods that were low in fat and cholesterol. Though he did try to adopt a low-fat diet, it was a challenge for him. He was a businessman, and had a very hectic schedule, and was unable to maintain a strict diet for long. Patel succeeded in losing weight but found that he had a difficult time with eating and decided to present this as an alternative. Throughout the years 2008 and 2009, the Lean and Green diet was planned and conceptualized.

The actual diet product was given a name – Lean and Green. The popular phrase that he used was, "Having Lean and Green is better than having no diet!" Patel worked upon the smaller plan of the diet – '5 & 1' that has been proved very effective by various researchers and dieticians. The five parts of the '5 & 1' program are small meals and consists of five portions of a specific food, while the sixth part of the program involves the consumption of carbohydrates for energy. It's a good idea to have the right amount of carbohydrates, which can spark weight loss.

The Lean and Green diet was soon ready to be launched in 2010. Priced at $70 for the selected starter kit, Lean and Green claims that they are the only one in the market offering a package including weight loss consultants and dieticians.

Chapter 1. Fundamentals of the Lean and Green diet

The Lean and Green diet is a practice that aims to reduce or maintain current weight. It is a diet that recommends eating a combination of processed foods called Fuellings and home-cooked meals (lean and Green meals). It is believed that it sticks to the brand product (input) and supplements it with meat, vegetables, and fatty snacks; this will keep you satisfied and nourished. At the same you don't need to worry much about losing muscles because you are eating enough protein and consuming too few calories. And that way, the individual who practices the diet can lose around 12 pounds in just 12 weeks using the ideal 5&1 weight plan.

In short, the Lean and Green n diet is a program that focuses on cutting calories and reducing carbohydrates in meals. To do this effectively, combine packaged foods called fuels with home-cooked meals, which encourages weight loss.

The Lean and Green diet encourages people to limit the number of calories that they should take daily. Under this program, dieters are encouraged to consume between 800 and 1000 calories daily. But unlike other types of commercial diet regimens, the Lean and Green diet comes in different variations. There are currently three variations of the Lean and Green diet plan that one can choose from according to one's needs.

- **5&1 Lean and Green diet Plan:** This is the most common version of the Lean and Green diet, and it involves eating five prepackaged meals from the Optimal Health Fuelings and one home-made balanced meal.

- **4&2&1 Octavia Diet Plan:** This diet plan is designed for people who want to have flexibility while following this regimen. Under this program, dieters are encouraged to eat more calories and have more flexible food choices. This means that they can consume 4 prepackaged Optimal Health Fuelings food, three home-cooked meals from the Lean and Green, and one snack daily.

- **5&2&2 Lean and Green diet Plan:** This diet plan is perfect for individuals who prefer to have a flexible meal plan in order to achieve a healthy weight. It is recommended for a wide variety of people. Under this diet regimen, dieters are required to eat 5 fuelings, 2 lean and Green meals, and 2 healthy snacks.

- **3&3 Lean and Green diet Plan:** This particular Diet plan is created for people who have moderate weight problems and merely want to maintain a healthy body. Under this diet plan, dieters are encouraged to consume 3 prepackaged Optimal Health Fuelings and three home-cooked meals.

- **Lean and Green for Nursing Mothers:** This diet regimen is designed for nursing mothers with babies of at least two months old. Aside from supporting breastfeeding mothers, it also encourages gradual weight loss.

- **Lean and Green for Diabetes:** This Lean and Green diet plan is designed for people who have Type 1 and Type 2 diabetes. The meal plans are designed so that dieters consume more green and lean meals, depending on their needs and condition.

- **Lean and Green forgout:** This diet regimen incorporates a balance of foods that are low in purines and moderate in protein.

- **Lean and Green for seniors (65 years and older):** Designed for seniors, this Lean and Green diet plan has some variations following the components of Fuelings depending on the needs and activities of the senior dieters.

- **Lean and Green for Teen Boys and Lean and Green for Teen girls (13-18 years old):** Designed for active teens, the Lean and Green for Teens Boys and Lean and Green for Teens girls provide the right nutrition to growing teens.

Regardless of which type of Lean and Green diet plan you choose, it is important that you talk with a coach to help you determine which plan is right for you based on your individual goals.

- **How to Start This Diet**

The Lean and Green diet is comprised of different phases. A certified coach will educate you on the steps that you need to undertake if you want to follow this regimen. below are some the things you need to know, especially when you are still starting with this diet regimen.

Initial Steps

During this phase, people are encouraged to consume800 to 1,000 calories to help you shed off at least 12 pounds within the next 12 weeks. For instance, if you are following the 5&1 Lean and Green diet Plan, then you need to eat 1 meal every 2 or 3 hours and include a 30-minute moderate workout most days of your week. You need to consume not more than 100grams of Carbs daily during this phase.

Further, consuming meals are highly encouraged. This phase also encourages the dieter to include 1 optional snack per day, such as ½ cup sugar-free gelatin, 3 celery sticks, and 12 ounces nuts. Aside from these things, below are other things that you need to remember when following this phase:

- Make sure that the portion size recommendations are for cooked weight and not the raw weight of your ingredients
- Opt for meals that are baked, grilled, broiled, or poached. Avoid frying foods, as this will increase your calorie intake.
- Eat at least 2 servings of fish rich in Omega-3 fatty acids. These include fishes like tuna, salmon, trout, mackerel, herring, and other cold-water fishes.
- Choose meatless alternatives like tofu and tempeh.
- Follow the program even when you are dining out. Keep in mind that drinking alcohol is discouraged when following this plan.

Maintenance Phase

As soon as you have attained your desired weight, the next phase is the transition stage. It is a 6-week stage that involves increasing your calorie intake to 1,550 per day. This is also the phase when you are allowed to add more varieties into your meal, such as wholegrains, low-fat dairy, and fruits.

After six weeks, you can now move into the 3&3 Lean and Green diet plan, so you are required to eat three Lean and Green meals and 3 Fueling foods.

Chapter 2. How does Lean and Green Work

The Lean and Green diet is viewed as a high-protein diet, with its protein having 10–35% of your daily calories. Be that as it may, the handled, powdered kind can prompt some not exactly beautiful outcomes. "The protein confine in addition to added substances can cause you to feel enlarged and have caused some undesirable Gi symptoms, making you off with unsweetened Greek yogurt for protein in a single smoothie," London says.

The FDA also doesn't direct dietary enhancements like shakes and powders for security and viability in a similar way it accomplishes for food. "Powders and protein 'mixes' may have unwanted fixings, or could interface with a drug you might be taking," London includes, "making it extra critical to ensure your doctor knows about you attempting the arrangement."

Like many commercial plans, Lean and Green involves buying most of the foods permitted on a diet in packaged form. The company deals on a wide range of food products that they call "fuelings"—on its website. These include pancakes, shakes, pasta dishes, soups, cookies, mashed potatoes, and popcorn.

Users pick the plan that best suits them. The 5 & 1 Plan entails eating five small meals per day. The meals can be selected from more than 60 substitutable fuelings, including one "lean and Green" meal, probably veggies or protein that you will prepare by yourself. The Optimal Essential Kit, costing $356.15, provides 119 servings, or about 20 days' worth.

Is Lean and Green and Medifast The Same?

Relatively, Medifast Inc. is known as the parent company of Lean and Green. It also the owner and the one that operates the Medifast program. The program is already present in the '80s and '90s with doctors who prescribe meals to their clients. Lean and Green makes use of identical foods with a similar macronutrient profile. Consumers can sign up online for the plan by themselves.

How Much Does Lean and Green Cost?

In comparison, the United States Department of Agriculture estimates that a woman whose ages range from 10-50 can follow a nutritious diet while spending as little as $166.40 per month on groceries. As long as she is preparing all her meals at home.

How Nutritious Is the Lean and Green diet?

Below is the breakdown comparison of meals' nutritional content on the Lean and Green I Weight 5&1 Plan and the federal government's 2015 Dietary guidelines for Americans.

	__Optimal Weight 5&1 Plan__	__Federal government Recommendation__
Calories	800-1,000	Men 19-25: 2,800 26-45: 2,600 46-65: 2,400 65+: 2,200 Women 19-25: 2,200 26-50: 2,000 51+: 1,800
__Total fat__ __% of Calorie Intake__	20%	20%-35%
__Total Carbohydrates__ __% of Calorie Intake__	40%	45%-65%
Sugars	10%-20%	N/A

<u>Fiber</u>	25g – 30g	Men 19-30: 34g. 31-50: 31g. 51+: 28g. Women 19-30: 28g. 31-50: 25g. 51+: 22g.
<u>Protein</u>	40%	10%-35%
<u>Sodium</u>	Under 2,300mg	Under 2,300mg.
<u>Potassium</u>	Average 3,000mg	At least 4,700mg.
<u>Calcium</u>	1,000mg – 1,200mg	Men 1,000mg. Women 19-50: 1,000mg. 51+: 1,200mg.

Chapter 3. The Benefits of the Lean and Green diet

Ideal for Portion Controllers - One of the hardest parts of the diet is learning to control portions and stick to them.

Practice long-term relationship with food: guiding the community to follow the Lean and Green diet can help improve a long-term positive relationship with food. Over time, you come to realize the types of foods you are allowed to eat and appreciate the healthy options you have.

No Responsibility Partner Needed: While some diets encourage you to make a friend to the diet, the Lean and Green diet is ideal for people who have no responsibility partners. The point is that people are connected to a community of dietitians who can provide the necessary support during the phases of this diet.

Better Overall Health - This particular diet is known to help improve overall well-being. In addition to weight loss, several studies have also shown that the Lean and Green diet can help people maintain blood sugar levels and stable blood pressure due to the limited sodium intake in food. In fact, Lean and Green provides less than 2,300 milligrams of sodium a day.

A Deeper Look into the Lean and Green diet

5&1 Lean and Green diet Plan: This is the most common version of the Lean and Green diet and it involves eating five prepackaged meals from the Optimal Health Fuelings and one home-made balanced meal.

4&2&1 Octavia Diet Plan: This diet plan is designed for people who want to have flexibility while following this regimen. Under this program, dieters are encouraged to eat more calories and have more flexible food choices. This means that they can consume 4 prepackaged Optimal Health Fuelings food, three home-cooked meals from the Lean and Green, and one snack daily.

5&2&2 Lean and Green diet Plan: This diet plan is perfect for individuals who prefer to have a flexible meal plan in order to achieve a healthy weight. It is recommended for a wide variety of people. Under this diet regimen, dieters are required to eat 5 fuelings, 2 lean and Green meals, and 2 healthy snacks.

3&3 Lean and Green diet Plan: This particular Diet plan is created for people who have moderate weight problems and merely want to maintain a healthy body. Under this diet plan, dieters are encouraged to consume 3 prepackaged Optimal Health Fuelings and three home-cooked meals.

Lean and Green for Nursing Mothers: This diet regimen is designed for nursing mothers with babies of at least two months old. Aside from supporting breastfeeding mothers, it also encourages gradual weight loss.

Lean and Green for Diabetes: This Lean and Green diet plan is designed for people who have Type 1 and Type 2 diabetes. The meal plans are designed so that dieters consume moregreen and lean meals depending on their needs and condition.

Lean and Green forgout: This diet regimen incorporates a balance of foods that are low in purines and moderate in protein.

Lean and Green for older people (65 years and older): Designed for seniors, this Lean and Green diet plan has some variations following the components of Fuelings depending on the needs and activities of the senior dieters.

Lean and Green for Teen Boys and Lean and Green for Teen girls (13-18 years old): Designed for active teens, the Lean and Green for Teens Boys and Lean and Green for Teens girls provide the right nutrition to growing teens.

Chapter 4. Recommended Foods and What to avoid in the Lean and Green diet

There are a lot many foods that you can eat while following the Lean and Green diet. However, you must know these foods by heart. This is particularly true if you are just new to this diet, and you have to follow the 5&1 Lean and Green diet Plan strictly. Thus, this section is dedicated to the types of foods that are recommended and those to avoid while following this diet regimen.

Recommended foods

There are numerous categories of foods that can be eaten under this diet regimen. This section will break down the Lean and Green foods that you can eat while following this diet regime.

Lean Foods

Leanest Foods - These foods are considered to be the leanest as it has only up to 4grams of total fat. Moreover, dieters should eat a 7-ounce cooked portion of these foods. Consume these foods with 1 healthy fat serving.

- **Fish:** Flounder, cod, haddock, grouper, Mahi, tilapia, tuna (yellowfin fresh or canned), and wild catfish.
- **Shellfish:** Scallops, lobster, crabs, shrimp
- **Game meat:** Elk, deer, buffalo
- **Ground turkey or other meat:** Should be 98% lean
- **Meatless alternatives:**14 egg whites, 2 cups egg substitute, 5 ounces seitan, 1 ½ cups 1% cottage cheese, and 12 ounces non-fat 0%greek yogurt

Leaner Foods - These foods contain 5 to 9grams of total fat. Consume these foods with 1 healthy fat serving. Make sure to consume only 6 ounces of a cooked portion of these foods daily:

- **Fish:** Halibut, trout, and swordfish
- **Chicken:** White meat such as breasts as long as the skin is removed
- **Turkey:** ground turkey as long as it is 95% to 97% lean.
- **Meatless options:**2 whole eggs plus 4 egg whites, 2 whole eggs plus one cup egg substitute, 1 ½ cups 2% cottage cheese, and 12 ounces low fat 2% plain Greek yogurt

Lean Foods - These are foods that contain 10g to 20g total fat. When consuming these foods, there should be no serving of healthy fat. These include the following:

- **Fish:** Tuna (Bluefin steak), salmon, herring, farmed catfish, and mackerel
- **Lean beef:** ground, steak, and roast
- **Lamb:** All cuts
- **Pork:** Pork chops, pork tenderloin, and all parts. Make sure to remove the skin
- **Ground turkey and other meats:**85% to 94% lean
- **Chicken:** Any dark meat
- **Meatless options:**15 ounces extra-firm tofu, 3 whole eggs (up to two times per week), 4 ounces reduced-fat skim cheese, 8 ounces part-skim ricotta cheese, and 5 ounces tempeh

Healthy Fat Servings - Healthy fat servings are allowed under this diet. They should contain 5grams of fat and less than grams of carbohydrates. Regardless of what type of Lean and Green diet plan you follow, make sure that you add between 0 and 2 healthy fat servings daily. Below are the different healthy fat servings that you can eat:

- 1 teaspoon oil (any kind of oil)
- 1 tablespoon low carbohydrate salad dressing
- 2 tablespoons reduced-fat salad dressing
- 5 to 10 black or green olives
- 1 ½ ounce avocado
- 1/3-ounce plain nuts including peanuts, almonds, pistachios

- 1 tablespoon plain seeds such as chia, sesame, flax, and pumpkin seeds
- ½ tablespoon regular butter, mayonnaise, and margarine

Green Foods

This section will discuss the green servings that you still need to consume while following the Lean and Green diet Plan. These include all kinds of vegetables that have been categorized from lower, moderate, and high in terms of carbohydrate content. One serving of vegetables should be at ½ cup unless otherwise specified.

Lower Carbohydrate - These are vegetables that contain low amounts of carbohydrates. If you are following the 5&1 Lean and Green diet plan, then these vegetables are good for you.

- A cup of green leafy vegetables, such as collard greens (raw), lettuce (green leaf, iceberg, butterhead, and romaine), spinach (raw), mustard greens, spring mix, bok choy (raw), and watercress.
- ½ cup of vegetables including cucumbers, celery, radishes, white mushroom, sprouts (mung bean, alfalfa), arugula, turnip greens, escarole, no pales, Swiss chard (raw), jalapeno, and bok choy (cooked).

Moderate Carbohydrate - These are vegetables that contain moderate amounts of carbohydrates. Below are the types of vegetables that can be consumed in moderation:

- **½ cup of any of the following vegetables** such as asparagus, cauliflower, fennel bulb, eggplant, portabella mushrooms, kale, cooked spinach, summer squash (zucchini and scallop).

Higher Carbohydrates - Foods that are under this category contain a high amount of starch. Make sure to consume limited amounts of these vegetables.

- **½ cup of the following vegetables** like chayote squash, red cabbage, broccoli, cooked collard and mustard greens, green or wax beans, kohlrabi, kabocha squash, cooked leeks, any peppers, okra, raw scallion, summer squash such as straight neck and crookneck, tomatoes, spaghetti squash, turnips, jicama, cooked Swiss chard, and hearts of palm.

Foods to avoid

The following foods are to be avoided, except it's included in the fuelings — they include:

- Fried foods: meats, fish, shellfish, vegetables, desserts like baked goods
- Refined grains: white bread, pasta, scones, hotcakes, flour tortillas, wafers, white rice, treats, cakes, cakes
- Certain fats: margarine, coconut oil, strong shortening
- Whole fat dairy: milk, cheddar, yogurt
- Alcohol: all varieties, no exception
- Sugar-sweetened beverages: pop, natural product juice, sports drinks, caffeinated drinks, sweet tea

The accompanying nourishments are beyond reach while on the 5&1 plan, however, included back during the 6-week progress stage and permitted during the 3&3 plan:

- Fruit: all kinds of fresh fruits
- Low fat or without fat dairy: yogurt, milk, cheddar

Chapter 5. What are the Fuelings, and how do They Work in your Body

The food items from Lean and Green are Lean and Green Fuelings. Classic Fuelings, Essential Fuelings, and Select Fuelings are available. All and all, you may pick from over 60 products that provide calories in your journey to reducing weight.

Lean and Green Fuelings includes 24 high-quality, full proteins, lactic acid bacteria minerals and vitamins, and no artificial colors, flavors, or sweeteners. Lean and Green Select Fuelings has global-inspired recipes. The brand also employs non-GMO ingredients obtained from all over the world. You will select from 13 bold varieties and foreign flavors such as Bolivian chia seeds, Mediterranean rosemary, and Indonesian cinnamon. Your calorie restriction program would dictate the number of Fuelings that you consume per day.

- Fuel is a ready-made product, so you don't have to make anything at mealtime.
- You will participate and save cash on the goods as a coach and market them to anyone if you like.
- Having 60 or so fuels to pick from implies that you might eventually get tired of having the same food again and again.
- Must buy from a distributor of the company.

They claim items and services have been suggested by and adopted for more than one million people for more than 20,000 clinicians. Nutritious, sweet, and efficient are Lean and Green Fuelings. At every point of the journey, they are clinically developed to have the best foods and are nutrient-dense, rightly portioned, and nutritionally compatible.

Through Lean and Green Fuelings, this may happen to many individuals; when you catch yourself losing the weight, make sure to keep it smooth and steady. Pros and Cons of Lean and Green diet

The Lean and Green diet depends on restrictive dinner substitution items and carefully calorie-controlled arranged suppers, so there's very little space for change.

The 5 and 1 plan limits calories to as low as 800-1000 every day, so it is not appropriate for women who are pregnant or individuals participating in exercise that require maximum physical activity.

Extraordinary calorie limitation can cause exhaustion, mind haze, cerebral pains, or menstrual changes. Al things considered, the 5 and 1 alternative ought not to be utilized long haul.

Be that as it May, the 3&3, and 4&2&1 Plan normally gracefully between 1100 to 2500 calories for every day and can be fitting to use for a more extended period.

After more than my 1-year journey in doing Lean and Green diet, these are the following pros and cons I have noticed:

Pros

Lean and Green 's program may be a solid match for you on the off chance that you need a diet plan that is clear and simple to follow, that will assist you with getting in shape rapidly, and offers worked in social help.

Accomplishes Rapid Weight Loss

Most solid individuals require around 1600 to 3000 calories for each day to keep up their weight. Limiting that number to as low as 800 basically ensure weight loss for a great many people.

Lean and Green 's 5&1 Plan is intended for brisk weight loss, making it a strong choice for somebody with a clinical motivation to shed pounds quick.

You enter the fat-loss stage in just 3 days. Look for Weight loss story on YouTube to see how many people out there are losing an impressing amount of weight, even 20 or more pounds in a week.

The average of 12 pounds in 12 weeks on the website counts all the people that do it by themselves, and nobody knows how many times they actually follow the plan, how many times they cheat, how much water they drink, exercise, etc.

Easy to Follow

As the diet depend on generally a prepackaged Fuelings, you are only accountable for doing one meal a day on the 5&1 Plan.

Moreover, each individual plan comes with meal logs and a sample meal plan to make it easier for the client to follow.

Although you are encouraged to make 1 to 3 Lean and Green foods a day, contingent on the strategy, they are very simple to make—because the program will include detailed recipes and a list of food options for you to choose from.

In addition, those who are not keen in cooking can purchase prepackaged meals called Flavors of Home to substitute for the Lean and Green meals.

Bundled Items Offer Comfort

In spite of the fact that you should search for your own elements for "lean and Green" dinners, the home conveyance choice for Lean and Green 's "Fuelings" spares time and vitality.

When the items show up, they're anything but difficult to get ready and make phenomenal snatch and go suppers.

Packaged Products

They will be delivered directly at home, and they are quick-to-made and grab-and-go.

Social Support and Coaching

Stay motivated, do not cheat. Point out how people on coaching achieve a much faster and more massive weight loss.

Offers Social Help

Social help is a crucial part of achievement with any weight loss plan. Lean and Green 's training project and gathering can give worked in consolation and backing for clients.

Lean and Green 's health coaches are available throughout the weight loss and maintenance programs.

It's Not a Ketogenic Diet

Carbs are allowed and higher than the majority of weight-loss diets out there, just not the refined ones.

No Counting Calories

You don't really need to count your calories when following this type of diet, just as long as you stick with the rule of Fuelings, meals, snacks and water intake depending on your preference may it be 5&1, 4&2&1 or 3&3.

Cons

There are additionally some potential drawbacks to Lean and Green 's plan, particularly on the off chance that you are stressed over cost, adaptability, and assortment.

It's Tough the First Weeks

You may feel hungry the first weeks; however, it will fade away soon.

Low calories

Even though lean and Green s diet plan emphasizes eating frequently throughout the day, each of its "Fuelings" only provides 110 calories. "Lean and Green" meals are also low in calories.

High Month-to-Month Cost

Lean and Green 's expense can be an obstacle for imminent clients.

The 5&1 plan goes in cost from $350 to $425 for 119 servings (around three weeks of dinner substitutions).

Subsequent to picking your arrangement, you'll buy the food. Costs fluctuate and rely upon the amount you're purchasing (and what). It's frequently most straightforward to get one of their units. The Essential Optimal Kit, which sets with the 5&1 Optimal weight Plan, accompanies 119 portions of food (counting shakes, sides, soups, bars, snacks, sides, and pasta) for only $414.60. The Optimal Health Kit for the 3&3 Plan offers 130 food servings of comparative things for $333.

Weight Loss May Not Be Sustainable

One challenge familiar to anyone on a diet is determining how to maintain weight loss once they have completed the program.

May Be Incompatible with Other Eating Plans

The Lean and Green diet incorporates specific projects for veggie lovers, individuals with diabetes, and breastfeeding ladies. Moreover, around 66% of its items are affirmed Sans gluten. In any case, alternatives are constrained for those on explicit diets.

For instance, Lean and Green Fuelings are not appropriate for veggie lovers or individuals with dairy hypersensitivities in light of the fact that most choices contain milk.

Moreover, the Fuelings utilize various fixings, so those with food hypersensitivities should peruse the names cautiously.

At long last, the Lean and Green program isn't suggested for pregnant ladies since it can't meet their dietary needs.

Chapter 6. Methods of Losing Weight with Lean and Green

Slimming with Substitute Meals According to the Lean and Green Method

Rules: eat every 2-3 hours and take a half hour / hour walk every day in the first phase. Below: half an hour of walking every day + 20 minutes of physical activity 2-3 times a week.

First stage.

In the first phase, 5 meals are made, one of which, nicknamed "Lean and Green", to be cooked at home.

Breakfast: replacement meal with a vegan vegetable protein smoothie, obtained by mixing a measuring cup of about 25-30grams in a glass of water. Coffee or tea can be added as long as it is without sugar but with stevia.

Snack: half a glass of meal replacement.

Lunch: a cucumber or a quarter of fennel + a glass of meal replacement.

Snack: like mid-morning.

Dinner. 120grams of chicken, veal or turkey breast, or omelette of 150grams of egg white + a slice of ham, or 120grams of white fish of your choice or 70grams of grilled tofu or seitan. Mixed salad with a teaspoon of oil, or grilled radicchio, spinach, Chinese cabbage, endive, escarole, chicory. Herbs and aromatic spices to taste.

An herbal tea sweetened with stevia.

The first phase should be continued until most of the weight is lost, and for about 2-8 weeks depending on how much you want to lose. The loss is approximately 6-7 pounds per month.

Second phase.

In the second phase, you have 6 meals a day, 4 of which with replacement meal, a "Lean and Green" meal to cook at home and 1 snack.

Breakfast: as in the first phase.

Mid-morning and afternoon snacks: as per the first phase.

Lunch and dinner: as in the first phase. At dinner you can vary the vegetables with mushrooms, courgettes, cucumbers, fennel, peppers, tomatoes.

Extra snack: 150grams of kiwi, oranges, pineapple, strawberries, red fruits, peach or 200grams of melon.

This phase is transitional, and is used to lose the last 2-4 pounds. It must last from 2 to 5 weeks.

The loss is about 3-4 pounds per month.

Third stage.

In the third phase, three meals a day with meal replacement are eaten, three normal meals. It is the maintenance phase.

As an alternative to meal replacements, I italicize what to eat.

Breakfast: as in the first phase, or 150grams of white skimmed yogurt + 3 shortbread biscuits or a pack of pavesini or two rusks with a little jam or a small banana. Or a homemade dessert of your choice with a maximum of 150 calories plus 150 ml of skimmed milk or sugar-free soy milk.

Snack: as in the first phase, or 200 ml of skimmed milk or 150 ml of unsweetened apple juice + 5 almonds.

Lunch: 60grams of pasta or rice or grains or legume pasta. 40grams of low-fat cheese between ricotta and primo sale, or a large egg or a small can of well-drained tuna in oil or 100grams of drained legumes in a jar. Simple sauce or 150grams of vegetables or vegetables of your choice. A teaspoon of oil.

Snack: as in the first phase, or 125grams of vitasnella / soy yogurt + a walnut or a small shortbread.

Dinner: as a Lean and Green dinner + a 25-gram slice of toast or 100grams of potatoes. Vegetables can vary according to your choice, in free quantity. Plus: 5grams of dark chocolate or 3 almonds and a sugar-free herbal tea.

Extra snack: 150grams of kiwi, oranges, pineapple, strawberries, red fruits, peach or 200grams of melon.

In the case of dinner out, lunch with the family, etcetera: the first phase is followed for all other meals and the sneaky dinner is considered as Lean and Green

Chapter 7. How the Lean and Green diet Can Help You Lose Weight

Lean and Green diet plans are suitable for all persons regardless of current age or weight. However, such factors will determine how long you will continue using the diet plan. Current age, weight, and overall health will also determine how well a person conforms to the dietary program.

The 2017 report funded by Medifast discovered that more than 70 percent of overweight adults who were placed on Medifast and received one-on-one behavioral support lost more than 5 percent of their body mass.

Following the Diet Plan

With the Lean and Green diet plan, you will enjoy more than 60 Fueling options. However, you will find it difficult to stop going on that diet. Also, you would get to take in more Lean and Green meal every time without taking stock of what you are consuming. This is because there are no sugars, points, or calories to record.

More studies showed that sticking to the Lean and Green diet plan is easy compared to other regular eating regimens. According to a 2008 study published in the Diabetes Educator, 16 out of 119 Medifast dietitians completed the eating regimen in 86 weeks. In contrast, only eight out of the 119 participants that tried regular diets were able to continue for 86 weeks.

Recipes are available on different online platforms. Besides, it is possible to have a complete Lean and Green meal for dinner. It is fast and cheap to order meals and cook them. Adherents can also depend on their LEAN and Green instructors and online forums for knowledge and techniques.

The official Pinterest page of Lean and Green is an excellent example of where beginners can get some tips on the best lean and Green meals. You can use the page as a conversion recipe guide to help you incorporate their ideas into your cooking plans.

Eating an all-out Lean and Green diet may be tough, but it is possible. The diet creators, Medifast group, recommend that you make a lean and Green lunch for a day. There are tips and ideas on how to go about this on the company's official webpage. The guide available on the page offers tips for selecting drinks and picking toppings with condiments. For example, ask for your steak (not more than 7-ounce) to be provided without herbal butter and replace the baked potato with steamed broccoli.

Picking an eating regimen and making orders is very easy. Medifast group offers automatic delivery. The only difficulty that will be experienced when cooking LEAN and Green meals involves the addition of water and microwave nuking. Any random person or regular cook should be able to make a lean and Green meal without much stress.

Medifast also states its diets have a healthy "fullness" level. This means that you can stay satisfied for a long time because of the high fiber and protein content. A 2010 report published on the Nutrition Journal observed that there are no significant discrepancies in satiety in post-meal or general fullness between the Lean and Green diet and other eating plans. The research on Diabetes Educator also found no significant association in dietary appetite across different types of diet. This is very important as specialists in nutrition have emphasized the relationship between satiety (the satisfying feeling you've had enough) and dietary plans.

Lean and Green diet from Medifast is ideal as the creators reveal that a panel tastes all their services before putting it on the market for their customers. The company also carries out different tracking of customer feedback regularly. Although this will not necessarily make the diet better than other dietary brands, the company believes it will satisfy their customers. LEAN and Green Fuelings do not involve artificial colors, sweeteners, or flavors.

Chapter 8. Sample 14-Day Meal Plan

Days	Breakfast	Lunch	Dinner	Snacks
1	Pumpkin & banana waffles	Yogurt garlic chicken	Zucchini salmon salad	Cucumber sandwich bites
2	Blueberry & cashew waffles	Lemony parmesan salmon	Pan fried salmon	Cucumber rolls
3	Cheddar and chive souffles	Easiest tuna cobbler ever	Grilled salmon with pineapple salsa	Olives and cheese stuffed tomatoes
4	Cheesy flax and hemp seeds muffins	Deliciously homemade pork buns	Mediterranean chickpea salad	Tomato salsa
5	Fantastic spaghetti squash with cheese and basil pesto	Mouthwatering tuna melts	Warm chorizo chickpea salad	Chili mango and watermelon salsa
6	Flaxseed porridge with cinnamon	Bacon wings	Greek roasted fish	Creamy spinach and shallots dip
7	Shirataki pasta with avocado and cream	Pepper pesto lamb	Tomato fish bake	Feta artichoke dip
8	Cinnamon pancakes with coconut	Tuna spinach casserole	Garlicky tomato chicken casserole	Avocado dip
9	Banana cashew toast	Greek style mini burger pies	Chicken cacciatore	Goat cheese and chives spread
10	Apple oatmeal	Family fun pizza	Fennel wild rice risotto	Veggie fritters
11	Strawberry yogurt treats	Lemony parmesan salmon	Wild rice prawn salad	White bean dip
12	Omega-3-rich cold banana breakfast	Tropical greens smoothie	Chicken broccoli salad with avocado dressing	Eggplant dip
13	Swiss chard and spinach with egg	Vitamin c smoothie cubes	Seafood paella	Bulgur lamb meatballs
14	Pumpkin & banana waffles	Overnight chocolate chia pudding	Herbed roasted chicken breasts	Cucumber bites

Chapter 9. Breakfast

Flaxseed Porridge with Cinnamon

Preparation Time: 10 minutes

Cooking Time: 5 minutes

Servings: 4

Ingredients:

- 1 tsp cinnamon
- 1½ tsp stevia
- 1 tbsp. unsalted butter
- 2 tbsp. flaxseed meal
- 2 tbsp. flaxseed oatmeal
- ½ cup shredded coconut
- 1 cup heavy cream
- 2 cups of water

Directions:

1. Take a medium pot, place it over low heat, add all the ingredients in it, stir until mixed and bring the mixture to boil.

2. When the mixture has boiled, remove the pot from heat, stir it well and divide it evenly between four bowls.

3. Let porridge rest for 10 minutes until slightly thicken and then serve.

Nutrition:

- Calories 171
- Total Fat 16g
- Total Carbs 6g
- Protein 2g

Swiss Chard and Spinach with Egg

Preparation Time: 5 minutes

Cooking Time: 10 minutes

Servings: 4

Ingredients:

- 4 egg whites
- 4 pieces of rice bread
- 20 pieces spinach leaves
- 20 pieces Swiss chard leaves
- 4 tbsp. parsley (fresh)
- 1 tsp. olive oil
- Sea salt, ground pepper, and dried mint

Directions:

1. Bring to a boil 2 cups of water in a pan just below the boiling point. Open an egg, separate the whites from the yolks. Put the whites in a small bowl. Lower the bowl towards the heated water, and gently pour the egg into the pan. Do the same with the other eggs. Poach the eggs for 4 minutes. After that, gently take the eggs, one at a time and transfer them into a plate. Do the same with the remaining 2 eggs.

2. Chop the parsley and sauté the leaves in a pan for 6 minutes. Toast the bread while doing this. When done, make a layer of the sautéed greens and the chopped parsley on top of the toasted rice bread. Put the poached eggs above the bed of greens. Sprinkle each serving with ground pepper, sea salt, and dried mint.

Nutrition:

- Calories: 49 kcal
- Protein: 5.31g
- Fat: 2.73g
- Carbohydrates: 0.48g

Omelette with Tomatoes and Spring Onions

Preparation Time: 5 minutes

Cooking Time: 20 minutes

Servings:

Ingredients:

- 6 eggs
- 2 tomatoes
- 2 spring onions
- 1 shallot
- 2 tbsp. butter
- 1 tbsp. olive oil
- 1 pinch of nutmeg
- salt
- pepper

Directions:

1. Whisk the eggs in a bowl.

2. Mix them together and season them with salt and pepper.

3. Peel the shallot and chop it up.

4. Clean the onions and cut them into rings.

5. Wash the tomatoes and cut them into pieces.

6. Heat butter and oil in a pan.

7. Braise half of the shallots in it.

8. Add half the egg mixture.

9. Let everything set over medium heat.

10. Scatter a few tomatoes and onion rings on top.

11. Repeat with the second half of the egg mixture.

12.   At the end, spread the grated nutmeg over the whole thing.

Nutrition:

- Kcal: 263
- Carbohydrates: 8g
- Protein: 20.3g
- Fat: 24g

Strawberry-Oat-Chocolate Chip Muffins

Preparation Time: 10 minutes
Cooking Time: 23 minutes
Servings: 12
Ingredients:

- 1¼ c. whole wheat pastry flour
- 1 c. rolled oats
- ¾ tsp. Baking soda
- ½ tsp. Baking powder
- ¼ tsp. salt
- 1 heaping cup bananas (about 2 to 3 large very ripe bananas)
- 1 tbsp. extra virgin olive oil
- 1 tbsp. honey or agave nectar
- 1 tsp. vanilla
- 1 egg
- 1 egg white
- 1/3 c. nonfat plain greek yogurt
- ½ c. unsweetened vanilla almond milk
- 1/3 c. mini chocolate chips
- 2/3 c. diced strawberries
- 12 thin slices of strawberries (about 3-4 strawberries) for garnish, if desired

Directions:

1.   Set the oven to 350°F and lightly grease a standard 12-cup muffin pan or grease with paper liners. In a large-sized mixing bowl, combine flour, oats, baking powder, baking soda, and salt. Stir to blend. Set aside the 2 tbsp. of the mixture.

2.   In a separate huge mixing bowl, combine together the mashed banana, olive oil, honey, and vanilla. Next, beat in the egg and egg white and beat until combined. Now add in greek yogurt and almond milk and beat with an electric mixer on low until smooth.

3.   Gradually put wet ingredients to dry ingredients and blend until just combined, but don't over mix the batter as it will make the muffins firm.

4.   Fill each muffin cup 2/3 full of batter. Gently tap the pan on the counter to even out the batter. Place a thin slice of strawberry onto each muffin, if desired.

Put the pan in the oven, then cook for 18 to 23 minutes, up to a toothpick place in the middle of the muffins, and comes out clean. Take off from the oven and let sit for 5 to 10 minutes in the pan before placing on a cooling rack.

Nutrition:

- Calories: 91 kcal
- Protein: 4.02g
- Fat: 2.63g
- Carbohydrates: 16.31g

Pumpkin & Banana Waffles

Preparation Time: 15 minutes
Cooking Time: 5 minutes
Servings: 4
Ingredients:

- ½ cup almond flour
- ½ cup coconut flour
- 1 tsp baking soda
- 1½ teaspoons ground cinnamon
- ¾ teaspoon groundginger
- ½ teaspoon ground cloves
- ½ teaspoon ground nutmeg
- Salt, to taste
- 2 tablespoons olive oil
- 5 large organic eggs
- ¾ cup almond milk
- ½ cup pumpkin puree
- 2 medium bananas, peeled and sliced

Directions:

1.   Preheat the waffle iron, and after that, grease it.

2.   In a sizable bowl, mix together flours, baking soda, and spices.

3.   In a blender, put the remaining ingredients and pulse till smooth.

4.   Add flour mixture and pulse till

5.   In preheated waffle iron, add the required quantity of mixture.

6.   Cook approximately 4-5 minutes.

7.   Repeat using the remaining mixture.

Nutrition:

- Calories: 357.2
- Fat: 28.5g
- Carbohydrates: 19.7g
- Fiber: 4g
- Protein: 14g

Oatmeal-Applesauce Muffins

Preparation Time: 15 minutes
Cooking Time: 25 minutes
Servings: 12
Ingredients:

- Topping
- 1/4 cup rolled oats
- 1 tbsp. brown sugar
- 1/8 tsp. cinnamon
- 1 tbsp. unsalted butter, melted
- Muffins
- 1 c. old fashioned rolled oats (not instant)
- 1 c. nonfat milk
- 1 c. whole wheat flour
- ½ c. brown sugar
- ½ c. unsweetened applesauce
- 2 egg whites
- 1 tsp. Baking powder
- ½ tsp. Baking soda
- ½ tsp. Salt
- ½ tsp. Cinnamon
- ½ tsp. sugar
- raisins or nuts (opt.)

Directions:

1. To begin, first, presoak the oats in milk for 1 hour,

2. Set the oven to 400°F then grease a standard 12-cup muffin pan with cooking spray or use paper liners.

3. In a mixing bowl, combine oat-milk mixture, applesauce, and egg whites. Blend well and set aside.

4. In a separate bowl, put together the whole wheat flour, brown sugar, baking powder, baking soda, salt, sugar, and cinnamon then mix.

5. Gradually put wet ingredients to dry ingredients and blend until just combined, but don't over mix the batter as it will make the muffins firm. Add raisins or nuts (opt.).

6. Prepare topping: In a small bowl, whisk together the oats, brown sugar, and cinnamon. Add in melted butter and toss gently with a fork to coat ingredients.

7. Fill each muffin cup 2/3 full of batter. Sprinkle topping on the top of each batter-filled muffin cup. Tap the pan gently on the counter to even out the batter. Place muffin pan in preheated oven and cook for 20 to 25 minutes or until a toothpick put in the middle of one of the muffins comes out clean. Take off from the oven and let sit for 5 minutes before serving.

Nutrition:

- Calories: 115 kcal
- Protein: 5.06g
- Fat: 2.57g
- Carbohydrates: 22.33g

Barley Breakfast Bowl with Lemon Yogurt Sauce

Preparation Time: 10 minutes
Cooking Time: 0 minutes
Servings: 2
Ingredients:

- 1½ c. cooked barley, keep warm
- 1 c. mung bean sprouts (or preferred variety)
- 1/3 c. Cotija cheese or queso fresco - crumbled
- ¼ c. sliced almonds, toasted
- ¼ tsp. kosher salt
- 1 small avocado – peeled/pitted, and flesh diced or sliced
- ½ tsp. Sea salt
- ¼ tsp. fresh ground black pepper
- Lemon Yogurt Sauce
- 1 c.greek plain yogurt
- 1 tsp. lemon zest, finely grated
- 1 tsp. Fresh lemon juice
- ¼ c. fresh mint or parsley, chopped
- Sea salt, to taste
- Fresh ground black pepper, to taste

Directions:

1. First, prepare the Lemon Yogurt Sauce: Combine the plain yogurt, lemon zest and juice, fresh mint or parsley, and salt & pepper in a bowl and stir to blend well. Cover and refrigerate until ready to serve.

2. Next, prepare the barley bowl: In a small mixing bowl, combine the barley, bean sprouts, cheese, almonds, and salt. Stir to mix well.

3. Divide barley mixture into 2 serving bowls. Top each barley bowl with 2 tbsp. lemon yogurt sauce and avocado. Put a pinch of salt and pepper to taste, serve, and enjoy!

Nutrition:

- Calories: 432 kcal
- Protein: 13.6g
- Fat: 23.37g
- Carbohydrates: 47.62g

Greek Yogurt with Cherry-Almond Syrup Parfait

Preparation Time: 25 minutes

Cooking Time: 5 minutes

Servings: 2

Ingredients:

- 1 c. fresh black or red cherries, pitted
- 2 tbsp. almond syrup
- 2 tbsp. coconut palm sugar
- 1 tsp. fresh-squeezed lemon juice
- 2 c.greek plain yogurt, stir to loosen
- 2 tbsp. sliced almonds, to garnish
- 4 tbsp. Granola of choice, to garnish (opt.)

Directions:

1. Place a saucepan over medium-high heat and combine cherries, almond syrup, sugar, lemon juice, and 1 tbsp. of water. Stir to combine, then place it to simmer, constantly stirring until sugar is dissolved. Continue to simmer for further 5 minutes, until liquid starts to turn into a syrupy mixture, but the cherries are still holding firm. Place the mixture to a bowl and let cool for 5 minutes at room temperature, then bring it in the refrigerator to chill until it is completely cold.

2. Place 1 cup of Greek yogurt into 2 serving bowls and spoon ½ of the cherries and their syrupy juices over the yogurt. Garnish with sliced almonds or granola, if desired. Serve immediately.

Nutrition:

- Calories: 185 kcal
- Protein: 4.75g
- Fat: 4.88g
- Carbohydrates: 33.07g

Omega-3-rich Cold Banana Breakfast

Preparation Time: 10 minutes

Cooking Time: 0 minutes

Servings: 2

Ingredients:

- ½ cup cold milk
- 4 tbsp. sesame seeds
- 2 tbsp. flaxseeds
- 4 tbsp. sunflower seeds
- 2 tbsp. Ground coconut
- 1 large sliced Banana

Directions:

1. Mix the milk and honey on your breakfast bowl. Use your coffee grinder to grind all the seeds. Add the ground seeds to the honey and milk mixture. Place the sliced bananas neatly on top. Sprinkle the ground coconuts for added flavor.

Nutrition:

- Calories: 393 kcal
- Protein: 14.85g
- Fat: 27.63g
- Carbohydrates: 27.37g

Fantastic Spaghetti Squash with Cheese and Basil Pesto

Preparation Time: 10 minutes

Cooking Time: 35 minutes

Servings: 2

Ingredients:

- 1 cup cooked spaghetti squash, drained
- Salt, to taste
- Freshly cracked black pepper, to taste
- ½ tbsp. olive oil
- ¼ cup ricotta cheese, unsweetened
- 2oz fresh mozzarella cheese, cubed
- 1/8 cup basil pesto

Directions:

1. Switch on the oven, then set its temperature to 375 °F and let it preheat.

2. Meanwhile, take a medium bowl, add spaghetti squash in it and then season with salt and black pepper.

3. Take a casserole dish, grease it with oil, add squash mixture in it, top it with ricotta cheese and mozzarella cheese and bake for 10 minutes until cooked.

4. When done, remove the casserole dish from the oven, drizzle pesto on top and serve immediately.

Nutrition:

- Calories 169
- Total Fat 11.3g
- Total Carbs 6.2g
- Protein 11.9g
- Sugar 0.1g
- Sodium 217mg

Banana-Oatmeal Vegan Pancakes

Preparation Time: 5 minutes

Cooking Time: 5 minutes

Servings: 12

Ingredients:

- 1¼ c. old fashioned oats
- ½ c. organic whole wheat flour
- 2 tsp. Baking powder

- ½ tsp. sea salt
- 1½ c. soymilk
- 2 ripe bananas

Directions:

1. To begin, heat griddle or skillet over medium heat.

2. Next, place all ingredients, except for banana, into a blender and process until smooth. Add the bananas to blender and blend until smooth.

3. Lightly grease griddle with olive or coconut oil, then pour ¼ c. of batter onto griddle and cook for at least 2 to 3 minutes, then flip and cook for about 2 minutes or up to the pancake is golden brown and cooked through.

4. Repeat process with remaining batter.

Nutrition:

- Calories: 59 kcal
- Protein: 3.49g
- Fat: 1.48g
- Carbohydrates: 11.52g

Pancakes with Berries

Preparation Time: 5 minutes
Cooking Time: 20 minutes
Servings: 2
Ingredients:

- Pancake:
- 1 egg
- 50g spelled flour
- 50g almond flour
- 15g coconut flour
- 150 ml of water
- salt

Filling:

- 40g mixed berries
- 10g chocolate
- 5g powdered sugar
- 4 tbsp. yogurt

Directions:

1. Put the flour, egg, and some salt in a blender jar.

2. Add 150 ml of water.

3. Mix everything with a whisk.

4. Mix everything into a batter.

5. Heat a coated pan.

6. Put in half of the batter.

7. Once the pancake is firm, turn it over.

8. Take out the pancake, add the second half of the batter to the pan and repeat.

9. Melt chocolate over a water bath.

10. Let the pancakes cool.

11. Brush the pancakes with the yogurt.

12. Wash the berry and let it drain.

13. Put berries on the yogurt.

14. Roll up the pancakes.

15. Sprinkle them with the powdered sugar.

16. Decorate the whole thing with the melted chocolate.

Nutrition:

- Kcal: 298
- Carbohydrates: 26g
- Protein: 21g
- Fat: 9g

Blueberry-Bran Breakfast Sundae

Preparation Time: 10 minutes
Cooking Time: 0 minutes
Servings: 2
Ingredients:

- 2 c. vanilla or lemon-flavored low-fat yogurt (preferably Greek yogurt) or flavor of choice.
- 2 c. bran flakes
- 1/4 c. fresh blueberries
- 2 tbsp. sliced almonds (or nuts of choice)
- 2 tbsp. chopped pecans (or nuts of choice)
- 2 tbsp. dried cranberries (or dried or fresh fruit of choice)

Directions:

1. In a bowl, place 1 c. yogurt, and one c. bran flakes.

2. Top with 1/8 c. fresh blueberries, followed by 1 tbsp. Each of sliced almonds, chopped pecans, and dried cranberries.

3. Repeat using the remaining ingredients to make a second serving. Serve immediately.

Nutrition:

- Calories: 420 kcal
- Protein: 21.12g
- Fat: 13.58g
- Carbohydrates: 59.8g

Huevos Rancheros

Preparation Time: 5 minutes
Cooking Time: 5 minutes
Servings: 2
Ingredients:

- (2) 8-inch whole wheat tortillas
- 2 hard-boiled eggs, sliced

- 2 slices of Canadian bacon or ham
- 1-ounce slice of cheddar cheese
- 2 tbsp. salsa

Directions:

1. Prepare the hardboiled eggs.

2. Put 1 tortilla on a plate, top with a slice of Canadian bacon or ham, the sliced egg, and a slice of cheddar cheese. Roll the tortilla up. Repeat with the remaining ingredients to prepare the second burrito.

3. Serve immediately with 1 tbsp. Salsa.

Nutrition:

- Calories: 741 kcal
- Protein: 36.12g
- Fat: 30.75g
- Carbohydrates: 79.37g

Millet Porridge

Preparation Time: 10 minutes
Cooking Time: 20 minutes
Servings: 2
Ingredients:

- Sea salt
- 1 tbsp. finely chopped coconuts
- 1/2 cup unsweetened coconut milk
- 1/2 cup rinsed and drained millet
- 1-1/2 cups alkaline water
- 3 drops liquid stevia

Directions:

1. Sauté the millet in a non-stick skillet for about 3 minutes.

2. Add salt and water then stir.

3. Let the meal boil then reduce the amount of heat.

4. Cook for 15 minutes then add the remaining ingredients. Stir.

5. Cook the meal for 4 extra minutes.

6. Serve the meal with toping of the chopped nuts.

Nutrition:

- Calories: 219 kcal
- Fat: 4.5g
- Carbs: 38.2g
- Protein: 6.4g

Cinnamon-Apple granola with Greek Yogurt

Preparation Time: 5 minutes
Cooking Time: 10 minutes

Servings: 2
Ingredients:

- 1/2 c. raw almonds, chopped (or raw nuts of choice)
- 1/2 c. raw walnuts, chopped (or raw nuts of choice)
- 1/2 apple, peeled and diced
- 1 tbsp. almond flour
- 2 tbsp. vanilla protein powder
- 1 tsp. Ground cinnamon
- 1/8 c. applesauce, unsweetened preferred
- 2 tsp. honey
- 2 tsp. almond butter
- 1/16 tsp. vanilla extract
- dash of sea salt
- 1 cup Greek plain or vanilla yogurt (or flavor of choice)

Directions:

1. In a mixing bowl, combine the chopped almonds, chopped walnuts (or preferred raw nuts), diced apple, vanilla protein powder, almond flour, lucuma (opt), and cinnamon and salt in a bowl. Mix well.

2. In a second bowl, combine the apple sauce, almond butter, honey, and vanilla extract. Mix well. Pour the bowl with the nuts into the bowl with the wet ingredients and blend together thoroughly. Make sure all dry ingredients get coated.

3. Place the granola mixture onto a parchment paper lined baking sheet and bake until the desired crunch is obtained approximately 8 to 10 minutes. Take off from oven and let cool or eat hot. Place 1/2 cup each Greek yogurt into two bowls. Divide the granola and sprinkle over the yogurt in each bowl. Serve immediately.

Nutrition:

- Calories: 312 kcal
- Protein: 11.72g
- Fat: 22.37g
- Carbohydrates: 19.92g

Apple Oatmeal

Preparation Time: 10 minutes
Cooking Time: 5 minutes
Servings: 2
Ingredients:

- 2/3 cups rolled oats
- 1 cup water
- 1 teaspoon ground cinnamon
- 1 cup of any non-fat milk, coconut milk or almond milk (optional)
- ¼ cup fresh apple juice

- 1 chopped apple, (unpeeled or peeled)

Directions:

1. Place the water, juice, and the apple in a deep pot. Bring to boil over medium heat.

2. Add the oats and cinnamon. Bring to another boil. Lower the heat temperature and let it simmer for 3 minutes or until it is thick.

3. Divide the serving into two and serve with milk.

Nutrition:

- Calories: 277 kcal
- Protein: 12.69g
- Fat: 7.69g
- Carbohydrates: 52.71g

Fried Egg with Bacon

Preparation Time: 5 minutes

Cooking Time: 10 minutes

Servings: 1

Ingredients:

- 2 eggs
- 30grams of bacon
- 2 tbsp. olive oil
- salt
- pepper

Directions:

1. Heat oil in the pan and fry the bacon.

2. Reduce the heat and beat the eggs in the pan.

3. Cook the eggs and season with salt and pepper.

4. Serve the fried eggs hot with the bacon.

Nutrition:

- Kcal: 405
- Carbohydrates: 1g
- Protein: 19g
- Fat: 38g

Cheddar and Chive Souffles

Preparation Time: 10 minutes

Cooking Time: 25 minutes

Servings: 8

Ingredients:

- ½ cup almond flour
- ¼ cup chopped chives
- 1 tsp salt
- ½ tsp xanthan gum
- 1 tsp ground mustard
- ¼ tsp cayenne pepper
- ½ tsp cracked black pepper

- ¾ cup heavy cream
- 2 cups shredded cheddar cheese
- ½ cup baking powder
- 6 organic eggs, separated

Directions:

1. Switch on the oven, then set its temperature to 350°F and let it preheat.

2. Take a medium bowl, add flour in it, add remaining ingredients, except for baking powder and eggs, and whisk until combined.

3. Separate egg yolks and egg whites between two bowls, add egg yolks in the flour mixture and whisk until incorporated.

4. Add baking powder into the egg whites and beat with an electric mixer until stiff peaks form and then stir egg whites into the flour mixture until well mixed.

5. Divide the batter evenly between eight ramekins and then bake for 25 minutes until done.

6. Serve straight away or store in the refrigerator until ready to eat.

Nutrition:

- Calories 288
- Total Fat 21g
- Total Carbs 3g
- Protein 14g

Chia Seedgel with Pomegranate and Nuts

Preparation Time: 5 minutes

Cooking Time: 10 minutes

Servings: 3

Ingredients:

- 20g hazelnuts
- 20g walnuts
- 120 ml almond milk
- 4 tbsp. chia seeds
- 4 tbsp. pomegranate seeds
- 1 teaspoon agave syrup
- Some lime juices

Directions:

1. Finely chop the nuts.

2. Mix the almond milk with the chia seeds.

3. Let everything soak for 10 to 20 minutes.

4. Occasionally stir the mixture with the chia seeds.

5. Stir in the agave syrup.

6. Pour 2 tablespoons of each mixture into a dessert glass.

7. Layer the chopped nuts on top.

8. Cover the nuts with 1 tablespoon each of the chia mass.

9. Sprinkle the pomegranate seeds on top and serve everything.

Nutrition:
- Kcal: 248
- Carbohydrates: 7g
- Protein: 1g
- Fat: 19g

Eel on Scrambled Eggs and Bread

Preparation Time: 5 minutes

Cooking Time: 10 minutes

Servings: 2

Ingredients:
- 4 eggs
- 1 shallot
- 4 slices of low carb bread
- 2 sticks of dill
- 200g smoked eel
- 1 tbsp. oil
- salt
- White pepper

Directions:

1. Mix the eggs in a bowl and season with salt and pepper.

2. Peel the shallot and cut it into fine cubes.

3. Chop the dill.

4. Remove the skin from the eel and cut it into pieces.

5. Heat the oil in a pan and steam the shallot in it.

6. Add in the eggs in and let them set.

7. Use the spatula to turn the eggs several times.

8. Reduce the heat and add the dill.

9. Stir everything.

10. Spread the scrambled eggs over four slices of bread.

11. Put the eel pieces on top.

12. Add some fresh dill and serve everything.

Nutrition:
- Kcal: 830
- Carbohydrates: 8g
- Protein: 45g
- Fat: 64g

Coconut Chia Pudding with Berries

Preparation Time: 20 minutes

Cooking Time: 45 minutes

Servings: 2

Ingredients:
- 150g raspberries and blueberries
- 60g chia seeds
- 500 ml coconut milk
- 1 teaspoon agave syrup
- ½ teaspoon ground bourbon vanilla

Directions:

1. Put the chia seeds, agave syrup, and vanilla in a bowl.

2. Pour in the coconut milk.

3. Mix thoroughly and let it soak for 30 minutes.

4. Meanwhile, wash the berries and let them drain well.

5. Divide the coconut chia pudding between two glasses.

6. Put the berries on top.

Nutrition:
- Kcal: 662
- Carbohydrates: 18g
- Protein: 8g
- Fat: 55g

Wholegrain Bread and Avocado

Preparation Time: 5 minutes

Cooking Time: 0 minutes

Serving: 1

Ingredients:
- 2 slices of whole meal bread
- 60g of cottage cheese
- 1 stick of thyme
- ½ avocado
- ½ lime
- Chili flakes
- salt
- pepper

Directions:

1. Cut the avocado in half.

2. Remove the pulp and cut it into slices.

3. Pour the lime juice over it.

4. Wash the thyme and shake it dry.

5. Remove the leaves from the stem.

6. Brush the whole wheat bread with the cottage cheese.

7. Place the avocado slices on top.

8. Top with the chili flakes and thyme.

9. Add salt and pepper and serve.

Nutrition:

- kcal: 490
- Carbohydrates: 31g
- Protein: 19g
- Fat: 21g

Omelette à la Margherita

Preparation Time: 10 minutes

Cooking Time: 20 minutes

Servings: 2

Ingredients:

- 3 eggs
- 50g parmesan cheese
- 2 tbsp. heavy cream
- 1 tbsp. olive oil
- 1 teaspoon oregano
- nutmeg
- salt
- pepper
- For covering:
- 3 - 4 stalks of basil
- 1 tomato
- 100ggrated mozzarella

Directions:

1. Mix the cream and eggs in a medium bowl.

2. Add the grated parmesan, nutmeg, oregano, pepper and salt and stir everything.

3. Heat the oil in a pan.

4. Add 1/2 of the egg and cream to the pan.

5. Let the omelette set over medium heat, turn it, and then remove it.

6. Repeat with the second half of the egg mixture.

7. Cut the tomatoes into slices and place them on top of the omelets.

8. Scatter the mozzarella over the tomatoes.

9. Place the omelets on a baking sheet.

10. Cook at 180 degrees for 5 to 10 minutes.

11. Then take the omelets out and decorate them with the basil leaves.

Nutrition:

- Kcal: 402
- Carbohydrates: 7g
- Protein: 21g
- Fat: 34g

Cinnamon Pancakes with Coconut

Preparation Time: 5 minutes

Cooking Time: 18 minutes

Servings: 2

Ingredients:

- 2 organic eggs
- 1 tbsp. almond flour
- 2oz cream cheese
- ¼ cup shredded coconut and more for garnishing
- ½ tbsp. erythritol
- 1/8 tsp salt
- 1 tsp cinnamon
- 4 tbsp. stevia
- ½ tbsp. olive oil

Directions:

1. Crack eggs in a bowl, beat until fluffy and then beat in flour and cream cheese until smooth.

2. Add remaining ingredients and then stir until well combined.

3. Take a frying pan, place it over medium heat, grease it with oil, then pour in half of the batter and cook for 3 to 4 minutes per side until the pancake has cooked and nicely golden brown.

4. Transfer pancake to a plate and cook another pancake in the same manner by using the remaining batter.

5. Sprinkle coconut on top of cooked pancakes and serve.

Nutrition:

- Calories 575
- Total Fat 51g
- Total Carbs 3.5g
- Protein 19g

Strawberry Yogurt treats

Preparation Time: 10 minutes

Cooking Time: 0 minutes

Servings: 2

Ingredients:

- 4 cups 0% fat plain yogurt
- 1 cup sliced strawberries
- 8 tbsp. of flax meal
- 4 tbsp. honey
- 8 tbsp. walnuts (chopped)

Directions:

1. Distribute 2 cups of the yogurt into your serving bowls. Neatly layer the flax meal and the walnut in the middle. Add a drizzle of half of the honey before

covering with the last layer of yogurt. Add the honey on top of the yogurt to add color when you serve.

Nutrition:

- Calories: 733 kcal
- Protein: 38.42g
- Fat: 30.57g
- Carbohydrates: 83.44g

Pumpkin Spice Quinoa

Preparation Time: 10 minutes

Cooking Time: 0 minutes

Servings: 2

Ingredients:

- 1 cup cooked quinoa
- 1 cup unsweetened coconut milk
- 1 large mashed banana
- 1/4 cup pumpkin puree
- 1 tsp. pumpkin spice
- 2 tsps. chia seeds

Directions:

1. In a container, mix all the ingredients.
2. Seal the lid then shake the container properly to mix.
3. Refrigerate overnight.
4. Serve.

Nutrition:

- Calories: 212 kcal
- Fat: 11.9g
- Carbs: 31.7g
- Protein: 7.3g

Alkaline Blueberry Spelt Pancakes

Preparation Time: 6 minutes

Cooking Time: 20 minutes

Servings: 3

Ingredients:

- 2 cups Spelt Flour
- 1 cup Coconut Milk
- 1/2 cup Alkaline Water
- 2 tbsps. grapeseed Oil
- 1/2 cup Agave
- 1/2 cup Blueberries
- 1/4 tsp. Sea Moss

Directions:

1. Mix the spelt flour, agave, grapeseed oil, hemp seeds, and the sea moss together in a bowl.

2. Add in 1 cup of hemp milk and alkaline water to the mixture, until you get the consistency mixture you like.

3. Crimp the blueberries into the batter.

4. Heat the skillet to moderate heat then lightly coat it with the grapeseed oil.

5. Pour the batter into the skillet then let them cook for approximately 5 minutes on every side.

6. Serve and Enjoy.

Nutrition:

- Calories: 203 kcal
- Fat: 1.4g
- Carbs: 41.6g
- Proteins: 4.8g

Smoothie Bowl with Spinach, Mango and Muesli

Preparation Time: 10 minutes

Cooking Time: 0 minutes

Servings: 1

Ingredients:

- 150g yogurt
- 30g apple
- 30g mango
- 30g low carb muesli
- 10g spinach
- 10g chia seeds

Directions:

1. Soak the spinach leaves and let them drain.
2. Peel the mango and cut it into strips.
3. Remove apple core and cut it into pieces.
4. Put everything except the mango together with the yogurt in a blender and make a fine puree out of it.
5. Put the spinach smoothie in a bowl.
6. Add the muesli, chia seeds, and mango.
7. Serve the whole thing

Nutrition:

- Kcal: 362
- Carbohydrates: 21g
- Protein: 12g
- Fat: 21g

Cheesy Spicy Bacon Bowls

Preparation Time: 10 minutes
Cooking Time: 22 minutes
Servings: 12
Ingredients:

- 6 strips Bacon, pan-fried until cooked but still malleable
- 4 eggs
- 60grams' cheddar cheese
- 40grams' cream cheese, grated
- 2 Jalapenos, sliced and seeds removed
- 2 tablespoons coconut oil
- ¼ teaspoon onion powder
- ¼ teaspoon garlic powder
- Dash of salt and pepper

Directions:

1. Preheat oven to 375 degrees Fahrenheit
2. In a bowl, beat together eggs, cream cheese, jalapenos (minus 6 slices), coconut oil, onion powder, garlic powder, and salt and pepper.
3. Using leftover bacon grease on a muffin tray, rubbing it into each insert. Place bacon-wrapped inside the parameters of each insert.
4. Pour beaten mixture halfway up each bacon bowl.
5. Garnish each bacon bowl with cheese and leftover jalapeno slices (placing one on top of each).
6. Leave in the oven for about 22 minutes, or until the egg is thoroughly cooked and cheese is bubbly.
7. Remove from oven and let cool until edible.
8. Enjoy!

Nutrition:

- Calories: 259
- Fat: 24g
- Carbs: 1g
- Fiber: 0g
- Protein: 10g

Yogurt with granola and Persimmon

Preparation Time: 5 minutes
Cooking Time: 5 minutes
Servings: 1
Ingredients:

- 150ggreek style yogurt
- 20g oatmeal
- 60g fresh persimmons
- 30 ml of tap water

Directions:

1. Put the oatmeal in the pan without any fat.
2. Toast them, stirring constantly, until golden brown.
3. Then put them on a plate and let them cool down briefly.
4. Peel the persimmon and put it in a bowl with the water. Mix the whole thing into a fine puree.
5. Put the yogurt, the toasted oatmeal, and the puree in layers in a glass and serve.

Nutrition:

- Kcal: 286
- Carbohydrates: 29g
- Protein: 1g
- Fat: 11g

Peanut Butter-Banana Muffins

Preparation Time: 15 minutes
Cooking Time: 25 minutes
Servings: 12
Ingredients:

- 1½ c. all-purpose flour
- 1 c. old-fashioned oats
- 1 tsp. Baking powder
- ½ tsp. Baking soda
- ½ tsp. salt
- 2 tbsp. Applesauce
- ¾ c. light brown sugar
- 2 large eggs
- 1 c. mashed banana (about 3 bananas)
- 6 tbsp. creamy peanut butter
- 1 c. low-fat buttermilk

Directions:

1. Bring a small nonstick skillet on medium heat and spray lightly with cooking spray. Add in the bell pepper and onion and sauté for 1 to 2 minutes, or until both are tender and the onion translucent.
2. In a small bowl, crack in eggs and whisk. Add in milk; whisk until well-blended. Pour eggs into the pan and cook, frequently stirring until eggs are scrambled to your liking.
3. To serve, spoon half the egg mixture into each tortilla, wrap, and serve. Try serving with a side of fresh fruit for a complete meal.

Nutrition:

- Calories: 187 kcal
- Protein: 8.12g
- Fat: 6.25g
- Carbohydrates: 27.82g

Jackfruit Vegetable Fry

Preparation Time: 5 minutes
Cooking Time: 5 minutes
Servings: 6
Ingredients:

- 2 finely chopped small onions
- 2 cups finely chopped cherry tomatoes
- 1/8 tsp. Ground turmeric
- 1 tbsp. olive oil
- 2 seeded and chopped red bell peppers
- 3 cups seeded and chopped firm jackfruit
- 1/8 tsp. cayenne pepper
- 2 tbsps. chopped fresh basil leaves
- Salt

Directions:

1. In a greased skillet, sauté the onions and bell peppers for about 5 minutes.
2. Add the tomatoes then stir.
3. Cook for 2 minutes.
4. Then add the jackfruit, cayenne pepper, salt, and turmeric.
5. Cook for about 8 minutes.
6. Garnish the meal with basil leaves.
7. Serve warm.

Nutrition:

- Calories: 236 kcal
- Fat: 1.8g
- Carbs: 48.3g
- Protein: 7g

Blueberry & Cashew Waffles

Preparation Time: 15 minutes
Cooking Time: 4-5 minutes
Servings: 5
Ingredients:

- 1 cup raw cashews
- 3 tablespoons coconut flour
- 1 tsp baking soda
- Salt, to taste
- ½ cup unsweetened almond milk
- 3 organic eggs
- ¼ cup coconut oil, melted
- 3 tablespoons organic honey
- ½ teaspoon organic vanilla flavor
- 1 cup fresh blueberries

Directions:

1. Preheat the waffle iron after which grease it.
2. In a mixer, add cashews and pulse till flour-like consistency forms.
3. Transfer the cashew flour in a big bowl.
4. Add almond flour, baking soda and salt and mix well.
5. In another bowl, put the remaining ingredients and beat till well combined.
6. Put the egg mixture into the flour mixture then mix till well combined.
7. Fold in blueberries.
8. In preheated waffle iron, add the required amount of mixture.
9. Cook for around 4-5 minutes.
10. Repeat with the remaining mixture.

Nutrition:

- Calories: 432
- Fat: 32
- Carbohydrates: 32g
- Protein: 13g

Shirataki Pasta with Avocado and Cream

Preparation Time: 10 minutes
Cooking Time: 6 minutes
Servings: 2
Ingredients:

- ½ packet of shirataki noodles, cooked
- ½ of an avocado
- ½ tsp cracked black pepper
- ½ tsp salt
- ½ tsp dried basil
- 1/8 cup heavy cream

Directions:

1. Place a medium pot half full with water over medium heat, bring it to boil, then add noodles and cook for 2 minutes.
2. Then drain the noodles and set aside until required.
3. Place avocado in a bowl, mash it with a fork,
4. Mash avocado in a bowl, transfer it in a blender, add remaining ingredients, and pulse until smooth.
5. Take a frying pan, place it over medium heat and when hot, add noodles in it, pour in the avocado mixture, stir well and cook for 2 minutes until hot.
6. Serve straight away.

Nutrition:

- Calories 131
- Total Fat 12.6g
- Total Carbs 4.9g

- Protein 1.2g
- Sugar 0.3g
- Sodium 588mg

Cream Cheese Egg Breakfast

Preparation Time: 5 minutes
Cooking Time: 5 minutes
Servings: 4
Ingredients:

- 2 eggs, beaten
- 1 tablespoon butter
- 2 tablespoons soft cream cheese with chives

Directions:

1. Melt the butter in a small skillet.
2. Add the eggs and cream cheese.
3. Stir and cook to desired doneness.

Nutrition:

- Calories: 341
- Fat: 31g
- Protein: 15g
- Carbohydrate: 0g
- Dietary Fiber: 3g

Cheesy Flax and Hemp Seeds Muffins

Preparation Time: 5 minutes
Cooking Time: 30 minutes
Servings: 2
Ingredients:

- 1/8 cup flax seeds meal
- ¼ cup raw hemp seeds
- ¼ cup almond meal
- Salt, to taste
- ¼ tsp baking powder
- 3 organic eggs, beaten
- 1/8 cup nutritional yeast flakes
- ¼ cup cottage cheese, low-fat
- ¼ cupgrated parmesan cheese
- ¼ cup scallion, sliced thinly
- 1 tbsp. olive oil

Directions:

1. Switch on the oven, then set it 360°F and let it preheat.
2. Meanwhile, take two ramekins, grease them with oil, and set aside until required.
3. Take a medium bowl, add flax seeds, hemp seeds, and almond meal, and then stir in salt and baking powder until mixed.

4. Crack eggs in another bowl, add yeast, cottage cheese, and parmesan, stir well until combined, and then stir this mixture into the almond meal mixture until incorporated.

5. Fold in scallions, then distribute the mixture between prepared ramekins and bake for 30 minutes until muffins are firm and the top is nicely golden brown.

6. When done, take out the muffins from the ramekins and let them cool completely on a wire rack.

7. For meal prepping, wrap each muffin with a paper towel and refrigerate for up to thirty-four days.

8. When ready to eat, reheat muffins in the microwave until hot and then serve.

Nutrition:

- Calories 179
- Total Fat 10.9g
- Total Carbs 6.9g
- Protein 15.4g
- Sugar 2.3g
- Sodium 311mg

Zucchini Muffins

Preparation Time: 10 minutes
Cooking Time: 25 minutes
Servings: 16
Ingredients:

- 1 tbsp. Ground flaxseed
- 3 tbsps. alkaline water
- 1/4 cup walnut butter
- 3 medium over-ripe bananas
- 2 small grated zucchinis
- 1/2 cup coconut milk
- 1 tsp. vanilla extract
- 2 cups coconut flour
- 1 tbsp. baking powder
- 1 tsp. cinnamon
- 1/4 tsp. sea salt

Directions:

1. Tune the temperature of your oven to 375ºF.
2. Grease the muffin tray with the cooking spray.
3. In a bowl, mix the flaxseed with water.
4. In a glass bowl, mash the bananas then stir in the remaining ingredients.
5. Properly mix and then divide the mixture into the muffin tray.
6. Bake it for 25 minutes.
7. Serve.

Nutrition:

- Calories: 127 kcal
- Fat: 6.6g
- Carbs: 13g
- Protein: 0.7g

Smoothie Bowl with Berries, Poppy Seeds, Nuts and Seeds

Preparation Time: 15 minutes
Cooking Time: 0 minutes
Servings: 2
Ingredients:

- 5 chopped almonds
- 2 chopped walnuts
- 1 apple
- ¼ banana
- 300g yogurt
- 60g raspberries
- 20g blueberries
- 20g rolled oats, roasted in a pan
- 10g poppy seeds
- 1 teaspoon pumpkin seeds
- Agave syrup

Directions:

1. Clean the fruit and let it drain.
2. Take some berries and set them aside.
3. Place the remaining berries in a tall mixing vessel.
4. Cut the banana into slices. Put a few aside.
5. Add the rest of the banana to the berries.
6. Remove the core of the apple and cut it into quarters.
7. Cut the quarters into thin wedges and set a few aside.
8. Add the remaining wedges to the berries.
9. Add the yogurt to the fruits and mix everything into a puree.
10. Sweeten the smoothie with the agave syrup.
11. Divide it into two bowls.
12. Serve it with the remaining fruit, poppy seeds, oatmeal, nuts and seeds.

Nutrition:

- Kcal: 284
- Carbohydrates: 21g
- Protein: 11g
- Fat: 19g

Crunchy Quinoa Meal

Preparation Time: 5 minutes
Cooking Time: 25 minutes
Servings: 2
Ingredients:

- 3 cups coconut milk
- 1 cup rinsed quinoa
- 1/8 tsp. Ground cinnamon
- 1 cup raspberry
- 1/2 cup chopped coconuts

Directions:

1. In a saucepan, pour milk and bring to a boil over moderate heat.
2. Add the quinoa to the milk and then bring it to a boil once more.
3. You then let it simmer for at least 15 minutes on medium heat until the milk is reduced.
4. Stir in the cinnamon then mix properly.
5. Cover it then cook for 8 minutes until the milk is completely absorbed.
6. Add the raspberry and cook the meal for 30 seconds.
7. Serve and enjoy.

Nutrition:

- Calories: 271 kcal
- Fat: 3.7g
- Carbs: 54g
- Proteins: 6.5g

Breakfast Pitas

Preparation Time: 4 minutes
Cooking Time: 6 minutes
Servings: 4
Ingredients:

- 8 egg whites
- 2 c. bell peppers, chopped (any color)
- 1 tsp. garlic powder
- 1 tsp. onion powder
- 1 c. raw spinach (cook if you prefer)
- 2 tsp. extra virgin olive oil
- 4 whole-wheat pita pockets

Directions:

1. Put the olive oil to a large sauté pan and place over medium heat. When the oil is hot in glistening, toss in the bell pepper and sauté for about 3 minutes or until tender. Add in the spinach now (if you want it cooked) and sauté for about 1 to 3 minutes or just up to the sides starts to wilt.

2. Place the egg whites into a small bowl, whisk well. Add in spices; whisk well. Pour the egg mixture into the sauté pan and scramble everything together.

3. Remove from heat and stuff ½ to 1 c. mixture into a pita pocket and serve.

Nutrition:

- Calories: 153 kcal
- Protein: 12.4g
- Fat: 3.41g
- Carbohydrates: 19.32g

Tasty Breakfast Donuts

Preparation Time: 5 minutes
Cooking Time: 5 minutes
Servings: 4
Ingredients:

- 43grams cream cheese
- 2 eggs
- 2 tablespoons almond flour
- 2 tablespoons erythritol
- 1 ½ tablespoons coconut flour
- ½ teaspoon baking powder
- ½ teaspoon vanilla extract
- 5 drops Stevia (liquid form)
- 2 strips bacon, fried until crispy

Directions:

1. Rub coconut oil over donut maker and turn on.

2. Mix all ingredients except bacon in a blender or food processor until smooth (should take around 1 minute).

3. Pour batter into donut maker, leaving 1/10 in each round for rising.

4. Leave for 3 minutes before flipping each donut. Leave for another 2 minutes or until a fork comes out clean when piercing them.

5. Take donuts out and let cool.

6. Repeat steps 1-5 until all batter is used.

7. Crumble bacon into bits and use to top donuts.

Nutrition:

- Calories: 60
- Fat: 5g
- Carbs: 1g
- Fiber: 0g
- Protein: 3g

Lavender Blueberry Chia Seed Pudding

Preparation Time: 1 hour 10 minutes
Cooking Time: 0 minutes

Servings: 4
Ingredients:

- 100g blueberries
- 70g organic quark
- 50g soy yogurt
- 30g hazelnuts
- 200 ml almond milk
- 2 tbsp. chia seeds
- 2 teaspoons agave syrup
- 2 teaspoons of lavender

Directions:

1. Bring the almond milk to a boil along with the lavender.

2. Let the mixture simmer for 10 minutes at a reduced temperature.

3. Let them cool down afterwards.

4. If the milk is cold, add the blueberries and puree everything.

5. Mix the whole thing with the chia seeds and agave syrup.

6. Let everything soak in the refrigerator for an hour.

7. Mix the yogurt and curd cheese together.

8. Add both to the crowd.

9. Divide the pudding into glasses.

10. Finely chop the hazelnuts and sprinkle them on top.

Nutrition:

- Kcal: 252
- Carbohydrates: 12g
- Protein: 1g
- Fat: 11g

Zucchini Pancakes

Preparation Time: 15 minutes
Cooking Time: 8 minutes
Servings: 8
Ingredients:

- 12 tbsps. alkaline water
- 6 large grated zucchinis
- Sea salt
- 4 tbsps. Ground Flax Seeds
- 2 tsps. olive oil
- 2 finely chopped jalapeño peppers
- 1/2 cup finely chopped scallions

Directions:

1. In a bowl, mix together water and the flax seeds then set it aside.

2. Pour oil in a large non-stick skillet then heat it on medium heat.

3. Then add the black pepper, salt, and zucchini.

4. Cook for 3 minutes then transfer the zucchini into a large bowl.

5. Add the flax seed and the scallion's mixture then properly mix it.

6. Preheat a griddle then grease it lightly with the cooking spray.

7. Pour 1/4 of the zucchini mixture into griddle then cook for 3 minutes.

8. Flip the side carefully then cook for 2 more minutes.

9. Repeat the procedure with the remaining mixture in batches.

10. Serve.

Nutrition:
- Calories: 71 kcal
- Fat: 2.8g
- Carbs: 9.8g
- Protein: 3.7g

Squash Hash

Preparation Time: 2 minutes

Cooking Time: 10 minutes

Servings: 2

Ingredients:
- 1 tsp. onion powder
- 1/2 cup finely chopped onion
- 2 cups spaghetti squash
- 1/2 tsp. sea salt

Directions:

1. Using paper towels, squeeze extra moisture from spaghetti squash.

2. Place the squash into a bowl then add the salt, onion, and the onion powder.

3. Stir properly to mix them.

4. Spray a non-stick cooking skillet with cooking spray then place it over moderate heat.

5. Add the spaghetti squash to pan.

6. Cook the squash for about 5 minutes.

7. Flip the hash browns using a spatula.

8. Cook for 5 minutes until the desired crispness is reached.

9. Serve.

Nutrition:
- Calories: 44 kcal
- Fat: 0.6g
- Carbs: 9.7g

- Protein: 0.9g

Avocado Red Peppers Roasted Scrambled Eggs

Preparation Time: 10 minutes

Cooking Time: 12 minutes

Servings: 3

Ingredients:
- 1/2 tablespoon butter
- Eggs, 2
- 1/2 roasted red pepper, about 1 1/2 ounces
- 1/2 small avocado, coarsely chopped, about 2 1/4 ounces
- Salt, to taste

Directions:

1. In a nonstick skillet, heat the butter over medium heat. Break the eggs into the pan and break the yolks with a spoon. Sprinkle with a little salt.

2. Stir to stir and continue stirring until the eggs start to come out. Quickly add the bell peppers and avocado.

3. Cook and stir until the eggs suit your taste. Adjust the seasoning, if necessary.

Nutrition:
- Calories: 317
- Fat: 26g
- Protein: 14g
- Dietary Fiber: 5g
- Net Carbs: 4g

Coconut Coffee and ghee

Preparation Time: 10 minutes

Cooking Time: 10 minutes

Servings: 5

Ingredients:
- ½ Tbsp. of coconut oil
- ½ Tbsp. of ghee
- 1 to 2 cups of preferred coffee (or rooibos or black tea, if preferred)
- 1 Tbsp. of coconut or almond milk

Directions:

1. Place the almond (or coconut) milk, coconut oil, ghee, and coffee in a blender (or milk frother).

2. Mix for around 10 seconds or until the coffee turns creamy and foamy.

3. Pour contents into a coffee cup.

4. Serve immediately and enjoy.

Nutrition:

- Calories: 150
- Total Fat: 15g
- Protein: 0g
- Total Carbs: 0g
- Net Carbs: 0g

Omega 3 Breakfast Shake

Preparation Time: 5 minutes
Cooking Time: 5 minutes
Servings: 2
Ingredients:

- 1 cup vanilla almond milk (unsweetened)
- 2 tablespoons blueberries
- 1 ½ tablespoons flaxseed meal
- 1 tablespoon MCT Oil
- ¾ tablespoon banana extract
- ½ tablespoon chia seeds
- 5 drops Stevia (liquid form)
- 1/8 tablespoon Xanthan gum

Directions:

1. In a blender, mix vanilla almond milk, banana extract, Stevia, and three ice cubes.
2. When smooth, add blueberries and pulse.
3. Once blueberries are thoroughly incorporated, add flaxseed meal and chia seeds.
4. Let sit for 5 minutes.
5. After 5 minutes, pulse again until all ingredients are nicely distributed. Serve and enjoy

Nutrition:

- Calories: 264
- Fats: 25g
- Carbs: 7g
- Protein: 4g

Lime Bacon Thyme Muffins

Preparation Time: 10 minutes
Cooking Time: 20 minutes
Servings: 3
Ingredients:

- 3 cups of almond flour
- 4 medium-sized eggs
- 1 cup of bacon bits
- 2 tsp. of lemon thyme
- ½ cup of melted ghee
- 1 tsp. of baking soda
- ½ tsp. of salt, to taste

Directions:

1. Pre-heat oven to 3500 F.
2. Put ghee in mixing bowl and melt.
3. Add baking soda and almond flour.
4. Put the eggs in.
5. Add the lemon thyme (if preferred, other herbs or spices may be used).
6. Drizzle with salt.
7. Mix all ingredients well.
8. Sprinkle with bacon bits
9. Line the muffin pan with liners.
10. Spoon mixture into the pan, filling the pan to about ¾ full.
11. Bake for about 20 minutes. Test by inserting a toothpick into a muffin. If it comes out clean, then the muffins are done.

Nutrition:

- Calories: 300
- Total Fat: 28g
- Protein: 11g
- Total Carbs: 6g
- Fiber: 3g

Porridge with Walnuts

Preparation Time: 5 minutes
Cooking Time: 10 minutes
Servings: 1
Ingredients:

- 50g raspberries
- 50g blueberries
- 25g ofground walnuts
- 20g of crushed flaxseed
- 10g of oatmeal
- 200 ml nut drink
- Agave syrup
- ½ teaspoon cinnamon
- salt

Directions:

1. Warm the nut drink in a small saucepan.
2. Add the walnuts, flaxseed, and oatmeal, stirring constantly.
3. Stir in the cinnamon and salt.
4. Simmer for 8 minutes.
5. Keep stirring everything.
6. Sweet the whole thing.
7. Put the porridge in a bowl.
8. Wash the berries and let them drain.
9. Add them to the porridge and serve everything.

Nutrition:

- Kcal: 378
- Carbohydrates: 11g
- Protein: 18g
- Fat: 27g

Banana Cashew Toast

Preparation Time: 10 minutes

Cooking Time: 0 minutes

Servings: 3

Ingredients:

- 1 cup roasted cashews (unsalted)
- 4 pieces oat bread
- 2 ripe medium-sized bananas
- Dash of salt
- Pinch of cinnamon
- 2 tsp. flax meals
- 2 tsp. honey

Directions:

1. Peel and slice the bananas into ½-inch pieces. Toast the bread. In a food processor, puree the salt and cashews until they are smooth. Use the puree as a spread on the toasts. On top of the spread, arrange a layer of bananas. Add flax meals and a dash of cinnamon on top of the bananas. Top the toast with honey.

Nutrition:

- Calories: 634 kcal
- Protein: 13.42g
- Fat: 47.6g
- Carbohydrates: 48.02g

Yummy Veggie Waffles

Preparation Time: 10 minutes

Cooking Time: 9 minutes

Servings: 3

Ingredients:

- 3 cups raw cauliflower, grated
- 1 cup cheddar cheese
- 1 cup mozzarella cheese
- ½ cup parmesan
- 1/3 cup chives, finely sliced
- 6 eggs
- 1 teaspoon garlic powder
- 1 teaspoon onion powder
- ½ teaspoon chili flakes
- Dash of salt and pepper

Directions:

1. Turn waffle maker on.

2. In a bowl, mix all the listed ingredients very well until incorporated.

3. Once the waffle maker is hot, distribute the waffle mixture into the insert.

4. Let cook for about 9 minutes, flipping at 6 minutes.

5. Remove from waffle maker and set aside.

6. Serve and enjoy!

Nutrition:

- Calories: 390
- Fat: 28g
- Carbs: 6g
- Fiber: 2g
- Protein: 30g

Alkaline Blueberry Muffins

Preparation Time: 5 Minutes

Cooking Time: 20 minutes

Servings: 3

Ingredients:

- 1 cup Coconut Milk
- 3/4 cup Spelt Flour
- 3/4 Teff Flour
- 1/2 cup Blueberries
- 1/3 cup Agave
- 1/4 cup Sea Mossgel
- 1/2 tsp. Sea Salt
- Grapeseed Oil

Directions:

1. Adjust the temperature of the oven to 365 degrees.

2. Grease 6 regular-size muffin cups with muffin liners.

3. In a bowl, mix together sea salt, sea moss, agave, coconut milk, and flourgel until they are properly blended.

4. You then crimp in blueberries.

5. Coat the muffin pan lightly with the grapeseed oil.

6. Pour in the muffin batter.

7. Bake for at least 30 minutes until it turns golden brown.

8. Serve.

Nutrition:

- Calories: 160 kcal
- Fat: 5g
- Carbs: 25g
- Proteins: 2g

Coconut Pancakes

Preparation Time: 5 minutes
Cooking Time: 15 minutes
Servings: 4
Ingredients:

- 1 cup coconut flour
- 2 tbsps. arrowroot powder
- 1 tsp. baking powder
- 1 cup coconut milk
- 3 tbsps. coconut oil

Directions:

1. In a medium container, mix in all the dry ingredients.
2. Add the coconut milk and 2 tbsps. of the coconut oil then mix properly.
3. In a skillet, melt 1 tsp. of coconut oil.
4. Pour a ladle of the batter into the skillet then swirl the pan to spread the batter evenly into a smooth pancake.
5. Cook it for like 3 minutes on medium heat until it becomes firm.
6. Turn the pancake to the other side then cook it for another 2 minutes until it turns golden brown.
7. Cook the remaining pancakes in the same process.
8. Serve.

Nutrition:

- Calories: 377 kcal
- Fat: 14.9g
- Carbs: 60.7g
- Protein: 6.4g

Quinoa Porridge

Preparation Time: 5 minutes
Cooking Time: 25 minutes
Servings: 2
Ingredients:

- 2 cups coconut milk
- 1 cup rinsed quinoa
- 1/8 tsp. Ground cinnamon
- 1 cup fresh blueberries

Directions:

1. In a saucepan, boil the coconut milk over high heat.
2. Add the quinoa to the milk then bring the mixture to a boil.
3. You then let it simmer for 15 minutes on medium heat until the milk is reducing.

4. Add the cinnamon then mix it properly in the saucepan.
5. Cover the saucepan and cook for at least 8 minutes until milk is completely absorbed.
6. Add in the blueberries then cook for 30 more seconds.
7. Serve.

Nutrition:

- Calories: 271 kcal
- Fat: 3.7g
- Carbs: 54g
- Protein: 6.5g

Banana Barley Porridge

Preparation Time: 15 minutes
Cooking Time: 5 minutes
Servings: 2
Ingredients:

- 1 cup divided unsweetened coconut milk
- 1 small peeled and sliced banana
- 1/2 cup barley
- 3 drops liquid stevia
- 1/4 cup chopped coconuts

Directions:

1. In a bowl, properly mix barley with half of the coconut milk and stevia.
2. Cover the mixing bowl then refrigerate for about 6 hours.
3. In a saucepan, mix the barley mixture with coconut milk.
4. Cook for about 5 minutes on moderate heat.
5. Then top it with the chopped coconuts and the banana slices.
6. Serve.

Nutrition:

- Calories: 159kcal
- Fat: 8.4g
- Carbs: 19.8g
- Proteins: 4.6g

Mushroom Quickie Scramble

Preparation Time: 10 minutes
Cooking Time: 10 minutes
Servings: 4
Ingredients:

- 3 small-sized eggs, whisked
- 4 pcs. Bella mushrooms
- ½ cup of spinach
- ¼ cup of red bell peppers

- 2 deli ham slices
- 1 tablespoon of ghee or coconut oil
- Salt and pepper to taste

Directions:

1. Chop the ham and veggies.
2. Put half a tbsp. of butter in a frying pan and heat until melted.
3. Sauté the ham and vegetables in a frying pan then set aside.
4. Get a new frying pan and heat the remaining butter.
5. Add the whisked eggs into the second pan while stirring continuously to avoid overcooking.
6. When the eggs are done, sprinkle with salt and pepper to taste.
7. Add the ham and veggies to the pan with the eggs.
8. Mix well.
9. Remove from burner and transfer to a plate.

Nutrition:

- Calories: 350
- Total Fat: 29g
- Protein: 21g
- Total Carbs: 5g

Goat, Cheese, Zucchini, and Kale Quiche

Preparation Time: 35 minutes
Cooking Time: 1 hour 10 minutes
Servings: 4
Ingredients:

- 4 large eggs
- 8 ounces fresh zucchini, sliced
- 10 ounces kale
- 3garlic cloves (minced)
- 1 cup of soy milk
- 1-ouncegoat cheese
- 1 cup grated parmesan
- 1 cup shredded cheddar cheese
- 2 teaspoons olive oil
- Salt and pepper, to taste

Directions:

1. Preheat oven to 350°F.
2. Heat 1 tsp of olive oil in a saucepan over medium-high heat. Sauté garlic for 1 minute until flavored.
3. Add the zucchini and cook for another 5-7 minutes until soft.
4. Beat the eggs and then add a little milk and Parmesan cheese.
5. Meanwhile, heat the remaining olive oil in another saucepan and add the kale. Cover and cook for 5 minutes until dry.
6. Slightly grease a baking dish with cooking spray and spread the kale leaves across the bottom. Add the zucchini and top with goat cheese.
7. Pour the egg, milk, and parmesan mixture evenly over the other ingredients. Top with cheddar cheese.
8. Bake for 50–60 minutes until golden brown. Check the center of the quiche, it should have a solid consistency.
9. Let chill for a few minutes before serving.

Nutrition:

- Total Carbohydrates: 15g
- Dietary Fiber: 2g
- Net Carbs: 13g
- Protein: 19g
- Total Fat: 18g
- Calories: 290

Tomato Braised Cauliflower with Chicken

Preparation Time: 10 minutes
Cooking Time: 30 minutes
Servings: 4
Ingredients:

- 4garlic cloves, sliced
- 3 scallions, to be trimmed and cut into 1-inch pieces
- ¼ teaspoon of dried oregano
- ¼ teaspoon of crushed red pepper flakes
- 4 ½ cups of cauliflower
- 1 ½ cups of diced canned tomatoes
- 1 cup of fresh basil, gently torn
- ½ teaspoon each of pepper and salt, divided
- 1 ½ teaspoon of olive oil
- 1 ½ lb. of boneless, skinless chicken breasts

Directions:

1. Get a saucepan and combine the garlic, scallions, oregano, crushed red pepper, cauliflower, and tomato, and add ¼ cup of water. Get everything boil together and add ¼ teaspoon of pepper and salt for seasoning, then cover the pot with a lid. Let it simmer for 10 minutes and stir as often as possible until you observe that the cauliflower is tender. Now, wrap up the seasoning with the remaining ¼ teaspoon of pepper and salt.

2. Toss the chicken breast with oil, olive preferably and let it roast in the oven with the heat of 450°F for 20 minutes and an internal temperature of 165°F. Allow the chicken to rest for like 10 minutes.

3. Now slice the chicken, and serve on a bed of tomato braised cauliflower.

Nutrition:

- Calories: 290
- Fat: 10g
- Carbohydrate: 13g
- Protein: 38g

Tomatillo and Green Chili Pork Stew

Preparation Time: 10 minutes
Cooking Time: 20 minutes
Servings: 4
Ingredients:

- 2 scallions, chopped
- 2 cloves of garlic
- 1 lb. tomatillos, trimmed and chopped
- 8 large romaine or green lettuce leaves, divided
- 2 serrano chilies, seeds, and membranes
- ½ tsp of dried Mexican oregano (or you can use regular oregano)
- 1 ½ lb. of boneless pork loin, to be cut into bite-sized cubes
- ¼ cup of cilantro, chopped
- ¼ tablespoon (each) salt and paper
- 1 jalapeno, seeds and membranes to be removed and thinly sliced
- 1 cup of sliced radishes
- 4 lime wedges

Directions:

1. Combine scallions, garlic, tomatillos, 4 lettuce leaves, serrano chilies, and oregano in a blender. Then puree until smooth

2. Put pork and tomatillo mixture in a medium pot. 1-inch of puree should cover the pork; if not, add water until it covers it. Season with pepper & salt, and cover it simmers. Simmer on heat for approximately 20 minutes.

3. Now, finely shred the remaining lettuce leaves.

4. When the stew is done cooking, garnish with cilantro, radishes, finely shredded lettuce, sliced jalapenos, and lime wedges.

Nutrition:

- Calories: 370
- Protein: 36g
- Carbohydrate: 14g
- Fat: 19g

Turkey Spinach Egg Muffins

Preparation Time: 10 minutes
Cooking Time: 20 minutes
Servings: 3
Ingredients:

- 5 egg whites
- 2 eggs
- ¼ cup cheddar cheese, shredded
- ¼ cup spinach, chopped
- ¼ cup milk
- 3 lean breakfast turkey sausage
- Pepper
- Salt

Directions:

1. Preheat the oven to 350 F. grease muffin tray cups and set aside.

2. In a pan, brown the turkey sausage links over medium-high heat until sausage is brown from all the sides.

3. Cut sausage in ½-inch pieces and set aside.

4. In a large bowl, whisk together eggs, egg whites, milk, pepper, and salt. Stir in spinach.

5. Pour egg mixture into the prepared muffin tray.

6. Divide sausage and cheese evenly between each muffin cup.

7. Bake in preheated oven for 20 minutes or until muffins are set.

8. Serve warm and enjoy.

Nutrition:

- Calories 123
- Fat 8g
- Carbs 9g
- Sugar 6g
- Protein 13g
- Cholesterol 123mg

Chicken Casserole

Preparation Time: 15 minutes

Cooking Time: 40 minutes

Servings: 4

Ingredients:

- 1 lb. cooked chicken, shredded
- ¼ cup greek yogurt
- 1 cup cheddar cheese, shredded
- ½ cup salsa
- 4 oz. cream cheese, softened
- 4 cups cauliflower florets
- 1/8 tsp black pepper
- ½ tsp kosher salt

Directions:

1. Add cauliflower florets into the microwave-safe dish and cook for 10 minutes or until tender.

2. Add cream cheese and microwave for 30 seconds more. Stir well.

3. Add chicken, yogurt, cheddar cheese, salsa, pepper, and salt and stir everything well.

4. Preheat the oven to 375 F.

5. Bake in preheated oven for 20 minutes.

6. Serve hot and enjoy.

Nutrition:

- Calories 429
- Fat 23g
- Carbs 6g
- Sugar 7g

- Protein 44g
- Cholesterol 149mg

Taco Zucchini Boats

Preparation Time: 20 minutes

Cooking Time: 55 minutes

Servings: 4

Ingredients:

- 4 medium zucchinis, cut in half lengthwise
- ¼ cup fresh cilantro, chopped
- ½ cup cheddar cheese, shredded
- ¼ cup water
- 4 oz. tomato sauce
- 2 tbsp. bell pepper, mined
- ½ small onion, minced
- ½ tsp oregano
- 1 tsp paprika
- 1 tsp chili powder
- 1 tsp cumin
- 1 tsp garlic powder
- 1 lb. lean ground turkey
- ½ cup salsa
- 1 tsp kosher salt

Directions:

1. Preheat the oven to 400 F.

2. Add ¼ cup of salsa in the bottom of the baking dish.

3. Using a spoon hollow out the center of the zucchini halves.

4. Chop the scooped-out flesh of zucchini and set aside ¾ of a cup chopped flesh.

5. Add zucchini halves in the boiling water and cook for 1 minute. Remove zucchini halves from water.

6. Add ground turkey in a large pan and cook until meat is no longer pink. Add spices and mix well.

7. Add reserved zucchini flesh, water, tomato sauce, bell pepper, and onion. Stir well and cover, simmer over low heat for 20 minutes.

8. Stuff zucchini boats with taco meat and top each with one tablespoon of shredded cheddar cheese.

9. Place zucchini boats in baking dish. Cover dish with foil and bake in preheated oven for 35 minutes.

10. Top with remaining salsa and chopped cilantro.

11. Serve and enjoy.

Nutrition:

- Calories 297
- Fat 17g
- Carbs 12g
- Sugar 3g
- Protein 30.2g
- Cholesterol 96mg

Parmesan Zucchini

Preparation Time: 15 minutes
Cooking Time: 15 minutes
Servings: 4
Ingredients:

- 4 zucchinis, quartered lengthwise
- 2 tbsp. fresh parsley, chopped
- 2 tbsp. olive oil
- ¼ tsp garlic powder
- ½ tsp dried basil
- ½ tsp dried oregano
- ½ tsp dried thyme
- ½ cup parmesan cheese, grated
- Pepper
- Salt

Directions:

1. Preheat the oven to 350 F. Line baking sheet with parchment paper and set aside.

2. In a small bowl, mix together parmesan cheese, garlic powder, basil, oregano, thyme, pepper, and salt.

3. Arrange zucchini onto the prepared baking sheet and drizzle with oil and sprinkle with parmesan cheese mixture.

4. Bake in preheated oven for 15 minutes then broil for 2 minutes or until lightly golden brown.

5. Garnish with parsley and serve immediately.

Nutrition:

- Calories 244
- Fat 14g
- Carbs 7g
- Sugar 5g
- Protein 15g
- Cholesterol 30mg

Avocado Lime Shrimp Salad

Preparation Time: 15 minutes
Cooking Time: 0 minutes
Servings: 2
Ingredients:

- 14 ounces of jumbo cooked shrimp, peeled and deveined; chopped
- 4 ½ ounces of avocado, diced
- 1 ½ cup of tomato, diced
- ¼ cup of chopped green onion
- ¼ cup of jalapeno with the seeds removed, diced fine
- 1 teaspoon of olive oil
- 2 tablespoons of lime juice
- 1/8 teaspoon of salt
- 1 tablespoon of chopped cilantro

Directions:

1. Get a small bowl and combine green onion, olive oil, lime juice, pepper, and a pinch of salt. Wait for about 5 minutes for all of them to marinate and mellow the flavor of the onion.

2. Get a large bowl and combined chopped shrimp, tomato, avocado, jalapeno. Combine all of the ingredients, add cilantro, and gently toss.

3. Add pepper and salt as desired.

Nutrition:

- Calories: 314
- Protein: 26g
- Carbs: 15g
- Fiber: 9g

Baked Cod & Vegetables

Preparation Time: 15 minutes
Cooking Time: 15 minutes
Servings: 4
Ingredients:

- 1 lb. cod fillets
- 8 oz. asparagus, chopped
- 3 cups broccoli, chopped
- ¼ cup parsley, minced
- ½ tsp lemon pepper seasoning
- ½ tsp paprika
- ¼ cup olive oil
- ¼ cup lemon juice
- 1 tsp salt

Directions:

1. Preheat oven to 400 F. Line a baking sheet with parchment paper and set aside.

2. In a small bowl, combine the lemon juice, paprika, olive oil, pepper spices, and salt.

3. Place the fish fillets in the center of the greaseproof paper. Arrange the broccoli and asparagus around the fish fillets.

4. Pour lemon juice mixture over the fish fillets and top with parsley.

5. Bake in preheated oven for 13-15 minutes.

6. Serve and enjoy.
Nutrition:
- Calories 240
- Fat 11g
- Carbs 6g
- Sugar 6g
- Protein 27g
- Cholesterol 56mg

Creamy Cauliflower Soup

Preparation Time: 15 minutes
Cooking Time: 15 minutes
Servings: 6
Ingredients:
- 5 cups cauliflower rice
- 8 oz. cheddar cheese, grated
- 2 cups unsweetened almond milk
- 2 cups vegetable stock
- 2 tbsp. water
- 1 small onion, chopped
- 2garlic cloves, minced
- 1 tbsp. olive oil
- Pepper
- Salt

Directions:
1. Heat olive oil in a large stockpot over medium heat.
2. Add onion and garlic and cook for 1-2 minutes.
3. Add cauliflower rice and water. Cover and cook for 5-7 minutes.
4. Now add vegetable stock and almond milk and stir well. Bring to boil.
5. Turn heat to low and simmer for 5 minutes.
6. Turn off the heat. Slowly add cheddar cheese and stir until smooth.
7. Season soup with pepper and salt.
8. Stir well and serve hot.

Nutrition:
- Calories 214
- Fat 15g
- Carbs 3g
- Sugar 3g
- Protein 16g
- Cholesterol 40mg

Healthy Broccoli Salad

Preparation Time: 25 minutes
Cooking Time: 0 minutes
Servings: 6
Ingredients:
- 3 cups broccoli, chopped
- 1 tbsp. apple cider vinegar
- ½ cup greek yogurt
- 2 tbsp. sunflower seeds
- 3 bacon slices, cooked and chopped
- 1/3 cup onion, sliced
- ¼ tsp stevia

Directions:
1. In a mixing bowl, mix together broccoli, onion, and bacon.
2. In a small bowl, mix together yogurt, vinegar, and stevia and pour over broccoli mixture. Stir to combine.
3. Sprinkle sunflower seeds on top of the salad.
4. Store salad in the refrigerator for 30 minutes.
5. Serve and enjoy.

Nutrition:
- Calories 90
- Fat 9g
- Carbs 4g
- Sugar 5g
- Protein 2g
- Cholesterol 12mg

Chicken Zucchini Noodles

Preparation Time: 20 minutes
Cooking Time: 5 minutes
Servings: 2
Ingredients:
- 1 large zucchini, spiralized
- 1 chicken breast, skinless & boneless
- ½ tbsp. jalapeno, minced
- 2garlic cloves, minced
- ½ tsp ginger, minced
- ½ tbsp. fish sauce
- 2 tbsp. coconut cream
- ½ tbsp. honey
- ½ lime juice
- 1 tbsp. peanut butter
- 1 carrot, chopped
- 2 tbsp. cashews, chopped
- ¼ cup fresh cilantro, chopped

- 1 tbsp. olive oil
- Pepper
- Salt

Directions:

1. Heat olive oil in a pan over medium-high heat.

2. Season chicken breast with pepper and salt. Once the oil is hot then add chicken breast into the pan and cook for 3-4 minutes per side or until cooked.

3. Remove chicken breast from pan. Shred chicken breast with a fork and set aside.

4. In a small bowl, mix together peanut butter, jalapeno, garlic, ginger, fish sauce, coconut cream, honey, and lime juice. Set aside.

5. In a large mixing bowl, combine together spiralized zucchini, carrots, cashews, cilantro, and shredded chicken.

6. Pour peanut butter mixture over zucchini noodles and toss to combine.

7. Serve immediately and enjoy.

Nutrition:

- Calories 353
- Fat 21g
- Carbs 20.5g
- Sugar 8g
- Protein 25g
- Cholesterol 54mg

Instant Pot Chipotle Chicken & Cauliflower Rice Bowls

Preparation Time: 10 minutes

Cooking Time: 20 minutes

Servings: 4

Ingredients:

- 1/3 cup of salsa
- 1 quantity of 14.5 oz. of can fire-roasted diced tomatoes
- 1 canned chipotle pepper + 1 teaspoon sauce
- ½ teaspoon of dried oregano
- 1 teaspoon of cumin
- 1 ½ lb. of boneless, skinless chicken breast
- ¼ teaspoon of salt
- 1 cup of reduced-fat shredded Mexican cheese blend
- 4 cups of frozen riced cauliflower
- ½ medium-sized avocado, sliced

Directions:

1. Combine the first ingredients in a blender and blend until they become smooth

2. Place the chicken in its pot and pour the sauce over it. Cover the lid and close the pressure valve. Put it on high heat for 20 minutes. Let the pressure release on its own before opening. Remove the piece and the chicken and then add it back to the sauce.

3. Microwave the riced cauliflower according to the directions on the package

4. Before you serve, divide the riced cauliflower, cheese, avocado, and chicken equally among the 4 bowls.

Nutrition:

- Calories: 287
- Protein: 35g
- Carbohydrate: 19g
- Fat: 12g

Broccoli Cheddar Breakfast Bake

Preparation Time: 10 minutes

Cooking Time: 45 minutes

Servings: 4

Ingredients:

- 9 eggs
- 6 cups of small broccoli florets
- ¼ teaspoon of salt
- 1 cup of unsweetened almond milk
- ¼ teaspoon of cayenne pepper
- ¼ teaspoon of ground pepper
- Cooking spray
- 4 oz. of shredded, reduced-fat cheddar

Directions:

1. Preheat your oven to about 375 degrees

2. In your large microwave-safe, add broccoli and 2 to 3 tablespoons of water. Microwave on high heat for 4 minutes or until it becomes tender. Now transfer the broccoli to a colander to drain excess liquid

3. Get a medium-sized bowl and whisk the milk, eggs, and seasonings together.

4. Set the broccoli neatly on the bottom of a lightly greased 13 x 9-inch baking dish. Sprinkle the cheese gently on the broccoli and pour the egg mixture on top of it.

5. Bake for about 45 minutes or until the center is set and the top forms a light brown crust.

Nutrition:

- Calories: 290
- Protein: 25g
- Carbohydrate: 8g
- Fat: 18g

Lean and Green Cloud Bread

Preparation Time: 25 minutes
Cooking Time: 35 minutes
Servings: 3
Ingredients:

- ½ cup of Fat-free 0% Plain Greek Yogurt (4.4 Oz)
- 3 Eggs, Separated
- 16 teaspoon Cream of Tartar
- 1 Packet sweetener (a granulated sweetener just like stevia)

Directions:

1. For about 30 minutes before making this meal, place the Kitchen Aid Bowl and the whisk attachment in the freezer.
2. Preheat your oven to 30 degrees
3. Remove the mixing bowl and whisk attachment from the freezer
4. Separate the eggs. Now put the egg whites in the Kitchen Aid Bowl, and they should be in a different medium-sized bowl.
5. In the medium-sized bowl containing the yolks, mix in the sweetener and yogurt.
6. In the bowl containing the egg white, add in the cream of tartar. Beat this mixture until the egg whites turn to stiff peaks.
7. Now, take the egg yolk mixture and carefully fold it into the egg whites. Be cautious and avoid over-stirring.
8. Place baking paper on a baking tray and spray with cooking spray.
9. Scoop out 6 equally-sized "blobs" of the "dough" onto the parchment paper.
10. Bake for about 25-35 minutes (make sure you check when it is 25 minutes, in some ovens, they are done at this timestamp). You will know they are done as they will get brownish at the top and have some crack.
11. Most people like them cold against being warm
12. Most people like to re-heat in a toast oven or toaster to get them a little bit crispy.
13. Your serving size should be about 2 pieces.

Nutrition:

- Calories: 234
- Protein: 23g
- Carbs: 5g
- Fiber: 8g
- Sodium: 223g

Sheet Pan Chicken Fajita Lettuce Wraps

Preparation Time: 15 minutes
Cooking Time: 30 minutes
Servings: 2
Ingredients:

- 1 lb. chicken breast, thinly sliced into strips
- 2 teaspoon of olive oil
- 2 bell peppers, thinly sliced into strips
- 2 teaspoon of fajita seasoning
- 6 leaves from a romaine heart
- Juice of half a lime
- ¼ cup plain of non-fat Greek yogurt

Directions:

1. Preheat your oven to about 400°F
2. Combine all of the ingredients except for lettuce in a large plastic bag that can be resealed. Mix very well to coat vegetables and chicken with oil and seasoning evenly.
3. Spread the contents of the bag evenly on a foil-lined baking sheet. Bake it for about 25-30 minutes, until the chicken is thoroughly cooked.
4. Serve on lettuce leaves and topped with Greek yogurt if you like

Nutrition:

- Calories: 387
- Fat: 6g
- Carbohydrate: 14g
- Protein: 18g

Braised Collard Greens in Peanut Sauce with Pork Tenderloin

Preparation Time: 20 minutes
Cooking Time: 1 hour 12 minutes
Servings: 4
Ingredients:

- 2 cups of chicken stock
- 12 cups of chopped collard greens
- 5 tablespoon of powdered peanut butter
- 3 cloves of garlic, crushed
- 1 teaspoon of salt
- ½ teaspoon of allspice
- ½ teaspoon of black pepper
- 2 teaspoon of lemon juice
- ¾ teaspoon of hot sauce
- 1 ½ lb. of pork tenderloin

Directions:

1. Get a pot with a tight-fitting lid and combine the collards with the garlic, chicken stock, hot sauce, and half of the pepper and salt. Cook on low heat for about 1 hour or until the collards become tender.

2. Once the collards are tender, stir in the allspice, lemon juice. And powdered peanut butter. Keep warm.

3. Season the pork tenderloin with the remaining pepper and salt, and broil in a toaster oven for 10 minutes when you have an internal temperature of 145°F. Make sure to turn the tenderloin every 2 minutes to achieve an even browning all over. After that, you can take away the pork from the oven and allow it to rest for like 5 minutes.

4. Slice the pork as you will

Nutrition:

- Calories: 320
- Fat: 10g
- Carbohydrate: 15g
- Protein: 45g

Savory Cilantro Salmon

Preparation Time: 10 minutes

Cooking Time: 30 minutes

Servings: 4

Ingredients:

- 2 tablespoons of fresh lime or lemon
- 4 cups of fresh cilantro, divided
- 2 tablespoon of hot red pepper sauce
- ½ teaspoon of salt. Divided
- 1 teaspoon of cumin
- 4, 7 oz. of salmon filets
- ½ cup of (4 oz.) water
- 2 cups of sliced red bell pepper
- 2 cups of sliced yellow bell pepper
- 2 cups of sliced green bell pepper
- Cooking spray
- ½ teaspoon of pepper

Directions:

1. Get a blender or food processor and combine half of the cilantro, lime juice or lemon, cumin, hot red pepper sauce, water, and salt; then puree until they become smooth. Transfer the marinade gotten into a large re-sealable plastic bag.

2. Add salmon to marinade. Seal the bag, squeeze out air that might have been trapped inside, turn to coat salmon. Refrigerate for about 1 hour, turning as often as possible.

3. Now, after marinating, preheat your oven to about 400°F. Arrange the pepper slices in a single layer in a slightly-greased, medium-sized square baking dish. Bake it for 20 minutes, turn the pepper slices once.

4. Drain your salmon and do away with the marinade. Crust the upper part of the salmon with the remaining chopped, fresh cilantro. Place salmon on the top of the pepper slices and bake for about 12-14 minutes until you observe that the fish flakes easily when it is being tested with a fork

5. Enjoy

Nutrition:

- Calories: 350
- Carbohydrate: 15g
- Protein: 42g
- Fat: 13g

Cheeseburger Soup

Preparation Time: 20 minutes

Cooking Time: 25 minutes

Servings: 4

Ingredients:

- ¼ cup of chopped onion
- 1 quantity of 14.5 oz. can dice tomato
- 1 lb. of 90% lean ground beef
- ¾ cup of diced celery
- 2 teaspoon of Worcestershire sauce
- 3 cups of low sodium chicken broth
- ¼ teaspoon of salt
- 1 teaspoon of dried parsley
- 7 cups of baby spinach
- ¼ teaspoon of ground pepper
- 4 oz. of reduced-fat shredded cheddar cheese

Directions:

1. Get a large soup pot and cook the beef until it becomes brown. Add the celery, onion, and sauté until it becomes tender. Remove from the fire and drain excess liquid.

2. Stir in the broth, tomatoes, parsley, Worcestershire sauce, pepper, and salt. Cover and allow it to simmer on low heat for about 20 minutes

3. Add spinach and leave it to cook until it becomes wilted in about 1-3 minutes. Top each of your servings with 1 ounce of cheese.

Nutrition:

- Calories: 400
- Carbohydrate: 11g
- Protein: 44g
- Fat: 20g

Tomato Cucumber Avocado Salad

Preparation Time: 15 minutes

Cooking Time: 0 minutes

Servings: 4

Ingredients:

- 12 oz. cherry tomatoes, cut in half
- 5 small cucumbers, chopped
- 3 small avocados, chopped
- ½ tsp ground black pepper
- 2 tbsp. olive oil
- 2 tbsp. fresh lemon juice
- ¼ cup fresh cilantro, chopped
- 1 tsp sea salt

Directions:

1. Add cherry tomatoes, cucumbers, avocados, and cilantro into the large mixing bowl and mix well.

2. Mix together olive oil, lemon juice, black pepper, and salt and pour over salad.

3. Toss well and serve immediately.

Nutrition:

- Calories 442
- Fat 31g
- Carbs 30.3g
- Sugar 4g
- Protein 2g
- Cholesterol 0mg

Salmon Florentine

Preparation Time: 5 minutes

Cooking Time: 30 minutes

Servings: 4

Ingredients:

- 1 ½ cups of chopped cherry tomatoes
- ½ cup of chopped green onions
- 2garlic cloves, minced
- 1 teaspoon of olive oil
- 1 quantity of 12 oz. package frozen chopped spinach, thawed and patted dry
- ¼ teaspoon of crushed red pepper flakes
- ½ cup of part-skim ricotta cheese
- ¼ teaspoon each for pepper and salt
- 4 quantities of 5 ½ oz. wild salmon fillets
- Cooking spray

Directions:

1. Preheat the oven to 350°F

2. Get a medium skillet to cook onions in oil until they start to soften, which should be in about 2 minutes. You can then add garlic inside the skillet and cook for an extra 1 minute. Add the spinach, red pepper flakes, tomatoes, pepper, and salt. Cook for 2 minutes while stirring. Remove the pan from the heat and let it cool for about 10 minutes. Stir in the ricotta

3. Put a quarter of the spinach mixture on top of each salmon fillet. Place the fillets on a slightly-greased rimmed baking sheet and bake it for 15 minutes or until you are sure that the salmon has been thoroughly cooked.

Nutrition:

- Calories: 350
- Carbohydrate: 15g
- Protein: 42g
- Fat: 13

Pesto Zucchini Noodles

Preparation Time: 15 minutes

Cooking Time: minutes 15 minutes

Servings: 4

Ingredients:

- 4 zucchinis, spiralized
- 1 tbsp. avocado oil
- 2garlic cloves, chopped
- 2/3 cup olive oil
- 1/3 cup parmesan cheese, grated
- 2 cups fresh basil
- 1/3 cup almonds
- 1/8 tsp black pepper
- ¾ tsp sea salt

Directions:

1. Add zucchini noodles into a colander and sprinkle with ¼ teaspoon of salt. Cover and let sit for 30 minutes. Drain zucchini noodles well and pat dry.

2. Preheat the oven to 400 F.

3. Place almonds on a parchment-lined baking sheet and bake for 6-8 minutes.

4. Transfer toasted almonds into the food processor and process until coarse.

5. Add olive oil, cheese, basil, garlic, pepper, and remaining salt in a food processor with almonds and process until pesto texture.

6. Heat avocado oil in a large pan over medium-high heat.

7. Add zucchini noodles and cook for 4-5 minutes.

8. Pour pesto over zucchini noodles, mix well and cook for 1 minute.

9. Serve immediately with baked salmon.

Nutrition:

- Calories: 525
- Fat 44g
- Carbs 3g
- Sugar 8g
- Protein 16g
- Cholesterol 30mg

Lemon Garlic Oregano Chicken with Asparagus

Preparation Time: 5 minutes

Cooking Time: 40 minutes

Servings: 4

Ingredients:

- 1 small lemon, juiced (this should be about 2 tablespoons of lemon juice)
- 1 ¾ lb. of bone-in, skinless chicken thighs
- 2 tablespoons of fresh oregano, minced
- 2 cloves of garlic, minced
- 2 lbs. of asparagus, trimmed
- ¼ teaspoon each or less for black pepper and salt

Directions:

1. Preheat the oven to about 350°F.

2. Put the chicken in a medium-sized bowl. Now, add the garlic, oregano, lemon juice, pepper, and salt and toss together to combine.

3. Roast the chicken in the air fryer oven until it reaches an internal temperature of 165°F in about 40 minutes. Once the chicken thighs have been cooked, remove and keep aside to rest.

4. Now, steam the asparagus on a stovetop or in a microwave to the desired doneness.

5. Serve asparagus with the roasted chicken thighs.

Nutrition:

- Calories: 350
- Fat: 10g
- Carbohydrate: 10g
- Protein: 32g

Rosemary Cauliflower Rolls

Preparation Time: 10 minutes

Cooking Time: 30 minutes

Servings: 3

Ingredients:

- 1/3 cup of almond flour
- 4 cups of riced cauliflower
- 1/3 cup of reduced-fat, shredded mozzarella or cheddar cheese
- 2 eggs
- 2 tablespoons of fresh rosemary, finely chopped
- ½ teaspoon of salt

Directions:

1. Preheat your oven to 400°F

2. Combine all the listed ingredients in a medium-sized bowl

3. Scoop cauliflower mixture into 12 evenly-sized rolls/biscuits onto a lightly-greased and foil-lined baking sheet.

4. Bake until it turns golden brown, which should be achieved in about 30 minutes.

Note: if you want to have the outside of the rolls/biscuits crisp, then broil for some minutes before serving.

Nutrition:

- Calories: 254
- Protein: 24g
- Carbohydrate: 7g
- Fat: 8g

Grilled Mahi with Jicama Slaw

Preparation Time: 20 minutes

Cooking Time: 10 minutes

Servings: 4

Ingredients:

- 1 teaspoon each for pepper and salt, divided
- 1 tablespoon of lime juice, divided
- 2 tablespoon + 2 teaspoons of extra virgin olive oil
- 4 raw mahi-mahi fillets, which should be about 8 oz. each
- ½ cucumber which should be thinly cut into long strips like matchsticks (it should yield
- about 1 cup)
- 1 jicama, which should be thinly cut into long strips like matchsticks (it should yield about 3 cups)
- 1 cup of alfalfa sprouts
- 2 cups of coarsely chopped watercress

Directions:

1. Combine ½ teaspoon of both pepper and salt, 1 teaspoon of lime juice, and 2 teaspoons of oil in a small bowl. Then brush the mahi-mahi fillets all through with the olive oil mixture.

2. Grill the mahi-mahi on medium-high heat until it becomes done in about 5 minutes, turn it to the other side, and let it be done for about 5 minutes. (You will have an internal temperature of about 145°F).

3. For the slaw, combine the watercress, cucumber, jicama, and alfalfa sprouts in a bowl. Now combine ½ teaspoon of both pepper and salt, 2 teaspoons of

ime juice, and 2 tablespoons of extra virgin oil in a small bowl. Drizzle it over slaw and toss together to combine.

Nutrition:

Calories: 320

Protein: 44g

Carbohydrate: 10g

Fat: 11g

Delicious Zucchini Quiche

Preparation Time: 25 minutes

Cooking Time: 1 hour

Servings: 8

Ingredients:

- 6 eggs
- 2 medium zucchinis, shredded
- ½ tsp dried basil
- 2garlic cloves, minced
- 1 tbsp. dry onion, minced
- 2 tbsp. parmesan cheese, grated
- 2 tbsp. fresh parsley, chopped
- ½ cup olive oil
- 1 cup cheddar cheese, shredded
- ¼ cup coconut flour
- ¾ cup almond flour
- ½ tsp salt

Directions:

1. Preheat oven to 350 F. grease 9-inch pie pan and set aside.

2. 2. Squeeze excess liquid from zucchini.

3. 3. Add all ingredients to large bowl and mix until well combined. Pour into prepared cake pan.

4. 4. Bake in a preheated oven for 45-60 minutes or until cooked through.

5. Remove from the oven and let it cool completely.

6. Slice and serve.

Nutrition:

- Calories 288
- Fat 23g
- Carbs 5g
- Sugar 6g
- Protein 11g
- Cholesterol 139mg

Green Bean Casserole

Preparation Time: 25 minutes
Cooking Time: 20 minutes
Servings: 4
Ingredients:

- 1 lb. fresh green beans, edges trimmed
- ½ oz. pork rinds, finely ground
- 1 oz. full-fat cream cheese
- ½ cup heavy whipping cream.
- ¼ cup diced yellow onion
- ½ cup chopped white mushrooms
- ½ cup chicken broth
- tbsp. unsalted butter.
- ¼ tsp. xanthan gum

Directions:

1 Over heat melt the butter in a skillet.

2 Sauté the onion and mushrooms until soft and fragrant, about 3-5 minutes.

3 Add the heavy cream, cream cheese, and broth to the skillet. Lightly beat until smooth. Boil and then simmer. Put the xanthan gum in the pan and remove from heat

4 Cut green beans into 2-inch pieces and place in 4-cup round pan. Pour sauce mixture over them and stir until covered. Fill the plate with ground pork rinds. Place in the fryer basket

5 Set the temperature to 320 degrees F and set the timer for 15 minutes. The top will be a golden and Green bean fork when fully cooked. Serve hot.

Nutrition:

- Calories: 267
- Protein: 3.6g
- Fat: 23.4g
- Carbs: 9.7g

Cabbage and Radishes Mix

Preparation Time: 20 minutes
Cooking Time: 15 minutes
Servings: 4
Ingredients:

- cups green cabbage; shredded
- ½ cup celery leaves; chopped.
- ¼ cup green onions; chopped.
- radishes; sliced
- tbsp. olive oil

- tbsp. balsamic vinegar
- ½ tsp. hot paprika
- 1 tsp. lemon juice

Directions:

1 In your air fryer's pan, combine all the ingredients and toss well.

2 Place the pan in the fryer and cook at 380°F for 15 minutes. Divide between plates and serve as a side dish

Nutrition:

- Calories: 130
- Fat: 4g
- Carbs: 4g
- Protein: 7g

Balsamic Cabbage

Preparation Time: 10 minutes
Cooking Time: 15 minutes
Servings: 4
Ingredients:

- cups red cabbage; shredded
- garlic cloves; minced
- 1 tbsp. olive oil
- 1 tbsp. balsamic vinegar
- Salt and black pepper to taste.

Directions:

1 In a pan that fits the air fryer, combine all the ingredients, toss, introduce the pan in the oven and cook at 380°F for 15 minutes

2 Divide between plates and serve as a side dish.

Nutrition:

- Calories: 151
- Fat: 2g
- Carbs: 5g
- Protein: 5g

Bok Choy and Butter Sauce

Preparation Time: 5 minutes
Cooking Time: 15 minutes
Servings: 4
Ingredients:

- bok choy heads; trimmed and cut into strips
- 1 tbsp. butter; melted
- tbsp. chicken stock
- 1 tsp. lemon juice
- 1 tbsp. olive oil

- A pinch of salt and black pepper

Directions:

1 In a pan that fits your air fryer, mix all the ingredients, toss, introduce the pan in the oven and cook at 380°F for 15 minutes.

2 Divide between plates and serve as a side dish

Nutrition:

- Calories: 141
- Fat: 3g
- Carbs: 4g
- Protein: 3g

Green Beans

Preparation Time: 5 minutes

Cooking Time: 20 minutes

Servings: 4

Ingredients:

- cups green beans; trimmed
- 1 tbsp. hot paprika
- tbsp. olive oil
- A pinch of salt and black pepper

Directions:

1 Take a bowl and mix the green beans with the other ingredients, toss, put them in the air fryer's basket and cook at 370°F for 20 minutes

2 Divide between plates and serve as a side dish.

Nutrition:

- Calories: 120
- Fat: 5g
- Carbs: 4g
- Protein: 2g

Kale Chips

Preparation Time: 10 minutes

Cooking Time: 5 minutes

Servings: 4

Ingredients:

- cups stemmed kale
- ½ tsp. salt
- tsp. avocado oil

Directions:

1 Take a large bowl, sprinkle the cabbage in avocado oil, and sprinkle with salt. Place in the fryer basket.

2 Set the temperature to 400 degrees F and set the timer for 5 minutes. The kale will be crispy when done. Serve immediately.

Nutrition:

- Calories: 25

- Protein: 0.5g
- Fat: 2.2g
- Carbs: 1.1g

Zucchini Spaghetti

Preparation Time: 20 minutes

Cooking Time: 15 minutes

Servings: 4

Ingredients:

- 1 lb. zucchinis, cut with a spiralizer
- 1 cup parmesan; grated
- ¼ cup parsley; chopped.
- ¼ cup olive oil
- garlic cloves; minced
- ½ tsp. red pepper flakes
- Salt and black pepper to taste.

Directions:

1 In a pan that fits your air fryer, mix all the ingredients, toss, introduce in the fryer and cook at 370°F for 15 minutes

2 Divide between plates and serve as a side dish.

Nutrition:

- Calories: 200
- Fat: 6g
- Carbs: 4g
- Protein: 5g

Parmesan Zucchini Rounds

Preparation Time: 25 minutes

Cooking Time: 20 minutes

Servings: 4

Ingredients:

- zucchinis; sliced
- 1 ½ cups parmesan; grated
- ¼ cup parsley; chopped.
- 1 egg; whisked
- 1 egg white; whisked
- ½ tsp. garlic powder
- Cooking spray

Directions:

1 Take a bowl and mix the egg with egg whites, parmesan, parsley and garlic powder and whisk.

2 Dredge each zucchini slice in this mix, place them all in your air fryer's basket, grease them with cooking spray and cook at 370°F for 20 minutes

3 Divide between plates and serve as a side dish.

Nutrition:

- Calories: 183

- Fat: 6g
- Fiber: 2g
- Carbs: 3g
- Protein: 8g

Coriander Artichokes

Preparation Time: 20 minutes
Cooking Time: 15 minutes
Servings: 4
Ingredients:

- 12 oz. artichoke hearts
- 1 tbsp. lemon juice
- 1 tsp. coriander, ground
- ½ tsp. cumin seeds
- ½ tsp. olive oil
- Salt and black pepper to taste.

Directions:

1 In a pan that fits your air fryer, mix all the ingredients, toss, introduce the pan in the fryer and cook at 370°F for 15 minutes

2 Divide the mix between plates and serve as a side dish.

Nutrition:

- Calories: 200
- Fat: 7g
- Carbs: 5g
- Protein: 8g

Turmeric Mushroom

Preparation Time: 5 minutes
Cooking Time: 15 minutes
Servings: 4
Ingredients:

- 1 lb. brown mushrooms
- garlic cloves; minced
- ¼ tsp. cinnamon powder
- 1 tsp. olive oil
- ½ tsp. turmeric powder
- Salt and black pepper to taste.

Directions:

1 In a bowl, combine all the ingredients and toss.

2 Put the mushrooms in your air fryer's basket and cook at 370°F for 15 minutes

3 Divide the mix between plates and serve as a side dish.

Nutrition:

- Calories: 208
- Fat: 7g

- Carbs: 5g
- Protein: 7g

Spinach and Artichokes Sauté

Preparation Time: 20 minutes
Cooking Time: 15 minutes
Servings: 4
Ingredients:

- 10 oz. artichoke hearts; halved
- cups baby spinach
- garlic cloves
- ¼ cup veggie stock
- tsp. lime juice
- Salt and black pepper to taste.

Directions:

1 In a pan that fits your air fryer, mix all the ingredients, toss, introduce in the fryer and cook at 370°F for 15 minutes

2 Divide between plates and serve as a side dish.

Nutrition:

- Calories: 209
- Fat: 6g
- Carbs: 4g
- Protein: 8g

Roasted Tomatoes

Preparation Time: 5 minutes
Cooking Time: 15 minutes
Servings: 4
Ingredients:

- tomatoes; halved
- ½ cup parmesan; grated
- 1 tbsp. basil; chopped.
- ½ tsp. onion powder
- ½ tsp. oregano; dried
- ½ tsp. smoked paprika
- ½ tsp. garlic powder
- Cooking spray

Directions:

1 Mix all the ingredients in a bowl and except the cooking spray and the parmesan.

2 Arrange the tomatoes in your air fryer's pan, sprinkle the parmesan on top and grease with cooking spray

3 Cook at 370°F for 15 minutes, divide between plates and serve.

Nutrition:

- Calories: 200

Fat: 7g

Carbs: 4g

Protein: 6g

Kale and Walnuts

Preparation Time: 5 minutes

Cooking Time: 15 minutes

Servings: 4

Ingredients:

- garlic cloves
- 10 cups kale; roughly chopped.
- 1/3 cup parmesan; grated
- ½ cup almond milk
- ¼ cup walnuts; chopped.
- 1 tbsp. butter; melted
- ¼ tsp. nutmeg, ground
- Salt and black pepper to taste.

Directions:

1 In a pan that fits the air fryer, combine all the ingredients, toss, introduce the pan in the machine and cook at 360°F for 15 minutes

2 Divide between plates and serve.

Nutrition:

- Calories: 160
- Fat: 7g

- Carbs: 4g
- Protein: 5g

Herbed Radish Sauté

Preparation Time: 5 minutes

Cooking Time: 15 minutes

Servings: 4

Ingredients:

- bunches red radishes; halved
- tbsp. parsley; chopped.
- tbsp. balsamic vinegar
- 1 tbsp. olive oil
- Salt and black pepper to taste.

Directions:

1 Take a bowl and mix the radishes with the remaining ingredients except the parsley, toss and put them in your air fryer's basket.

2 Cook at 400°F for 15 minutes, divide between plates, sprinkle the parsley on top and serve as a side dish

Nutrition:

- Calories: 180
- Fat: 4g
- Carbs: 3g
- Protein: 5g

Feta Artichoke Dip

Preparation Time: 10 minutes
Cooking Time: 30 minutes
Servings: 8
Ingredients:

- 8 ounces artichoke hearts, drained and quartered
- ¾ cup basil, chopped
- ¾ cup green olives, pitted and chopped
- 1 cup parmesan cheese, grated
- 5 ounces feta cheese, crumbled

Directions:

1. In your food processor, mix the artichokes with the basil and the rest of the ingredients, pulse well, and transfer to a baking dish.

2. Introduce in the oven, bake at 375° F for 30 minutes and serve as a party dip.

Nutrition:

- Calories 186;
- Fat 12.4g;
- Fiber 0.9g;
- Carbs 2.6g;
- Protein 1.5g

Avocado Dip

Preparation Time: 5 minutes
Cooking Time: 0 minutes
Servings: 8
Ingredients:

- ½ cup heavy cream
- 1green chili pepper, chopped
- Salt and pepper to the taste
- 4 avocados, pitted, peeled and chopped
- 1 cup cilantro, chopped
- ¼ cup lime juice

Directions:

1. In a blender, combine the cream with the avocados and the rest of the ingredients and pulse well.

2. Divide the mix into bowls and serve cold as a party dip.

Nutrition:

- Calories 200;
- Fat 14.5g;
- Fiber 3.8g;
- Carbs 8.1g;

- Protein 7.6g

Marinated Eggs

Preparation Time: 2 hours and 10 minutes
Cooking Time: 7 minutes
Servings: 4
Ingredients:

- 6 eggs
- 1 and ¼ cups water
- ¼ cup unsweetened rice vinegar
- 2 tablespoons coconut aminos
- Salt and black pepper to the taste
- 2garlic cloves, minced
- 1 teaspoon stevia 4 ounces cream cheese
- 1 tablespoon chives, chopped

Directions:

1. Put the eggs in a pot, add water to cover, bring to a boil over medium heat, cover and cook for 7 minutes.

2. Rinse eggs with cold water and leave them aside to cool down.

3. In a bowl, mix one cup water with coconut aminos, vinegar, stevia, and garlic and whisk well.

4. Put the eggs in this mix, cover with a kitchen towel, and leave them aside for 2 hours, rotating from time to time.

5. Peel eggs, cut in halves, and put egg yolks in a bowl.

6. Add ¼ cup water, cream cheese, salt, pepper, and chives and stir well.

7. Stuff egg whites with this mix and serve them.

8. Enjoy!

Nutrition:

- Calories: 289 kcal
- Protein: 15.86g
- Fat: 22.62g
- Carbohydrates: 4.52g
- Sodium: 288mg

Eggplant Dip

Preparation Time: 10 minutes
Cooking Time: 40 minutes
Servings: 4
Ingredients:

- 1 eggplant, poked with a fork
- 2 tablespoons tahini paste
- 2 tablespoons lemon juice

- 2garlic cloves, minced
- 1 tablespoon olive oil
- Salt and black pepper to the taste
- 1 tablespoon parsley, chopped

Directions:

1. Put the eggplant in a roasting pan, bake at 400° F for 40 minutes, cool down, peel and transfer to your food processor.

2. Add the rest of the ingredients except the parsley, pulse well, divide into small bowls and serve as an appetizer with the parsley sprinkled on top.

Nutrition:

- Calories 121;
- Fat 4.3g;
- Fiber 1g;
- Carbs 1.4g;
- Protein 4.3g

Chicken and Mushrooms

Preparation Time: 10 minutes
Cooking Time: 15 minutes
Servings: 6
Ingredients:

- 2 chicken breasts
- 1 cup of sliced white champignons
- 1 cup of sliced green chilies
- 1/2 cup scallions hacked
- 1 teaspoon of chopped garlic
- 1 cup of low-fat cheddar shredded cheese (1-1,5 lb. grams fat / ounce)
- 1 tablespoon of olive oil
- 1 tablespoon of butter

Directions:

1. Fry the chicken breasts with olive oil.

2. When needed, salt and pepper.

3. Grill breasts of chicken in a plate with grill.

4. For every serving, weigh 4 ounces of chicken. (Make two servings, save leftovers for another meal).

5. In a butter pan, stir in mushrooms, green peppers, scallions, and garlic until smooth, and a little dark.

6. Place the chicken in a baking platter.

7. Cover with mushroom combination.

8. Top on ham.

9. Place the cheese in a 350 oven until it melts.

Nutrition:

- Carbohydrates: 2g
- Protein: 23g
- Fat: 11g
- Cholesterol: 112mg
- Sodium: 198mg
- Potassium: 261mg

Veggie Fritters

Preparation Time: 10 minutes
Cooking Time: 10 minutes
Servings: 4
Ingredients:

- 2garlic cloves, minced
- 2 yellow onions, chopped
- 4 scallions, chopped
- 2 carrots, grated
- 2 teaspoons cumin, ground
- ½ teaspoon turmeric powder
- Salt and black pepper to the taste
- ¼ teaspoon coriander, ground
- 2 tablespoons parsley, chopped
- ¼ teaspoon lemon juice
- ½ cup almond flour
- 2 beets, peeled and grated
- 2 eggs, whisked
- ¼ cup tapioca flour
- 3 tablespoons olive oil

Directions:

1. In a bowl, combine the garlic with the onions, scallions and the rest of the ingredients except the oil, stir well and shape medium fritters out of this mix.

2. Heat up a pan with the oil over medium-high heat, add the fritters, cook for 5 minutes on each side, arrange on a platter and serve.

Nutrition:

- Calories 209;
- Fat 11.2g;
- Fiber 3g;
- Carbs 4.4g;
- Protein 4.8g

Tomato Salsa

Preparation Time: 5 minutes
Cooking Time: 0 minutes
Servings: 6
Ingredients:

- 1garlic clove, minced
- 4 tablespoons olive oil

- 5 tomatoes, cubed
- 1 tablespoon balsamic vinegar
- ¼ cup basil, chopped
- 1 tablespoon parsley, chopped
- 1 tablespoon chives, chopped
- Salt and black pepper to the taste
- Pita chips for serving

Directions:

1. In a bowl, mix the tomatoes with the garlic and the rest of the ingredients except the pita chips, stir, divide into small cups and serve with the pita chips on the side.

Nutrition:

- Calories 160;
- Fat 13.7g;
- Fiber 5.5g;
- Carbs 10.1g;
- Protein 2.2

Pesto Crackers

Preparation Time: 10 minutes

Cooking Time: 17 minutes

Servings: 6

Ingredients:

- ½ teaspoon baking powder
- Salt and black pepper to the taste
- 1 and ¼ cups almond flour
- ¼ teaspoon basil, dried 1garlic clove, minced
- 2 tablespoons basil pesto
- A pinch of cayenne pepper
- 3 tablespoons ghee

Directions:

1. In a bowl, mix salt, pepper, baking powder, and almond flour.

2. Add garlic, cayenne, and basil and stir.

3. Add pesto and whisk.

4. Also, add ghee and mix your dough with your finger.

5. Spread this dough on a lined baking sheet, introduce in the oven at 325 degrees F and bake for 17 minutes.

6. Leave aside to cool down, cut your crackers, and serve them as a snack.

7. Enjoy!

Nutrition:

- Calories: 9 kcal
- Protein: 0.41g
- Fat: 0.14g
- Carbohydrates: 1.86g

- Sodium: 2mg

goat Cheese and Chives Spread

Preparation Time: 10 minutes

Cooking Time: 0 minute

Servings: 4

Ingredients:

- 2 ounces goat cheese, crumbled
- ¾ cup sour cream
- 2 tablespoons chives, chopped
- 1 tablespoon lemon juice
- Salt and black pepper to the taste
- 2 tablespoons extra virgin olive oil

Directions:

1. In a bowl, mix the goat cheese with the cream and the rest of the ingredients and whisk really well.

2. Keep in the fridge for 10 minutes and serve as a party spread.

Nutrition:

- Calories 220;
- Fat 11.5g;
- Fiber 4.8g;
- Carbs 8.9g;
- Protein 5.6g

Bacon Cheeseburger

Preparation Time: 10 minutes

Cooking Time: 30 minutes

Servings: 4

Ingredients:

- 1 lb. lean ground beef
- 1/4 cup chopped yellow onion
- 1 clove garlic, minced
- 1 tbsp. yellow mustard
- 1 tbsp. Worcestershire sauce
- 1/2 tsp. salt
- Cooking spray
- 4 ultra-thin slices cheddar cheese, cut into 6 equal-sized rectangular pieces
- 3 pieces of turkey bacon, each cut into 8 evenly-sized rectangular pieces
- 24 dill pickle chips
- 4-6green leaf
- Lettuce leaves, torn into 24 small square-shaped pieces
- 12 cherry tomatoes, sliced in half

Directions:

1. Pre-heat oven to 400°F.

2. Combine the garlic, salt, onion, Worcestershire sauce, and beef in a medium-sized bowl, and mix well.

3. Form mixture into 24 small meatballs.

4. Put meatballs onto a foil-lined baking sheet and cook for 12-15 minutes.

5. Leave oven on.

6. Top every meatball with a piece of cheese, then go back to the oven until cheese melts for about 2 to 3 minutes.

7. Let meatballs cool.

8. To assemble bites: on a toothpick layer a cheese-covered meatball, piece of bacon, piece of lettuce, pickle chip, and a tomato half.

Nutrition:

- Fat: 14g
- Cholesterol: 41mg
- Carbohydrates: 30g
- Protein: 15g

Wrapped Plums

Preparation Time: 5 minutes

Cooking Time: 0 minutes

Servings: 8

Ingredients:

- 2 ounces prosciutto, cut into 16 pieces
- 4 plums, quartered
- 1 tablespoon chives, chopped
- A pinch of red pepper flakes, crushed

Directions:

1. Wrap each plum quarter in a prosciutto slice, arrange them all on a platter, sprinkle the chives and pepper flakes all over and serve.

Nutrition:

- Calories 30;
- Fat 1g;
- Fiber 0g;
- Carbs 4g;
- Protein 2g

Olives and Cheese Stuffed Tomatoes

Preparation Time: 10 minutes

Cooking Time: 0 minutes

Servings: 24

Ingredients:

- 24 cherry tomatoes, top cut off and insides scooped out
- 2 tablespoons olive oil
- ¼ teaspoon red pepper flakes
- ½ cup feta cheese, crumbled
- 2 tablespoons black olive paste
- ¼ cup mint, torn

Directions:

1. In a bowl, mix the olives paste with the rest of the ingredients except the cherry tomatoes and whisk well.

2. Stuff the cherry tomatoes with this mix, arrange them all on a platter and serve as an appetizer.

Nutrition:

- Calories 136;
- Fat 8.6g;
- Fiber 4.8g;
- Carbs 5.6g;
- Protein 5.1g

Chili Mango and Watermelon Salsa

Preparation Time: 5 minutes

Cooking Time: 0 minutes

Servings: 12

Ingredients:

- 1 red tomato, chopped
- Salt and black pepper to the taste
- 1 cup watermelon, seedless, peeled and cubed
- 1 red onion, chopped
- 2 mangos, peeled and chopped
- 2 chili peppers, chopped
- ¼ cup cilantro, chopped
- 3 tablespoons lime juice
- Pita chips for serving

Directions:

1. In a bowl, mix the tomato with the watermelon, the onion and the rest of the ingredients except the pita chips and toss well.

2. Divide the mix into small cups and serve with pita chips on the side.

Nutrition:

- Calories 62;
- Fat 4g;
- Fiber 1.3g;
- Carbs 3.9g;
- Protein 2.3g

White Bean Dip

Preparation Time: 10 minutes
Cooking Time: 0 minute
Servings: 4
Ingredients:

- 15 ounces canned white beans, drained and rinsed
- 6 ounces canned artichoke hearts, drained and quartered
- 4garlic cloves, minced
- 1 tablespoon basil, chopped
- 2 tablespoons olive oil
- Juice of ½ lemon
- Zest of ½ lemon, grated
- Salt and black pepper to the taste

Directions:

1. In your food processor, combine the beans with the artichokes and the rest of the ingredients except the oil and pulse well.
2. Add the oil gradually, pulse the mix again, divide into cups and serve as a party dip.

Nutrition:

- Calories 274;
- Fat 11.7g;
- Fiber 6.5g;
- Carbs 18.5g;
- Protein 16.5g

Cheeseburger Pie

Preparation Time: 20 minutes
Cooking Time: 90 minutes
Servings: 4
Ingredients:

- 1 large spaghetti squash
- 1 lb. lean ground beef
- 1/4 cup diced onion
- 2 eggs
- 1/3 cup low-fat, plain Greek yogurt
- 2 tbsp. tomato sauce
- 1/2 tsp. Worcestershire sauce
- 2/3 cup reduced-fat, shredded cheddar cheese
- 2 oz. dill pickle slices
- Cooking spray

Directions:

1. Preheat oven to 400°F. Slice spaghetti squash in half lengthwise; dismiss pulp and seeds.
2. Spray insides with cooking spray.
3. Place squash halves cut-side- down onto a foil-lined baking sheet, and bake for 30 minutes.
4. Once cooked, let cool to before scraping squash flesh with a fork to remove spaghetti-like strands; set aside.
5. Push squash strands in the bottom and up sides of the greased pie pan, creating an even layer.
6. Meanwhile, set up pie filling.
7. In a lightly greased, medium-sized skillet, cook beef and onion over medium heat 8 to 10 minutes, sometimes stirring, until meat is brown.
8. Drain and remove from heat.
9. In a medium-sized bowl, whisk together eggs, tomato paste, Greek yogurt, and Worcestershire sauce. Stir inground beef mixture.
10. Pour pie filling over squash crust.
11. Sprinkle meat filling with cheese, and then top with dill pickle slices.
12. Bake for 40 minutes.

Nutrition:

- Calories: 409 Cal
- Fat: 24.49g
- Carbohydrates: 15.06g
- Protein: 30.69g

Cucumber Rolls

Preparation Time: 5 minutes
Cooking Time: 0 minutes
Servings: 6
Ingredients:

- 1 big cucumber, sliced lengthwise
- 1 tablespoon parsley, chopped
- 8 ounces canned tuna, drained and mashed
- Salt and black pepper to the taste
- 1 teaspoon lime juice

Directions:

1. Arrange cucumber slices on a working surface, divide the rest of the ingredients, and roll.
2. Arrange all the rolls on a platter and serve as an appetizer.

Nutrition:

- Calories 200
- Fat 6g
- Fiber 3.4g
- Carbs 7.6g
- Protein 3.5g

Pumpkin Muffins

Preparation Time: 10 minutes

Cooking Time: 15 minutes

Servings: 18

Ingredients:

- ¼ cup sunflower seed butter
- ¾ cup pumpkin puree
- 2 tablespoons flaxseed meal
- ¼ cup coconut flour
- ½ cup erythritol
- ½ teaspoon nutmeg, ground
- 1 teaspoon cinnamon, ground
- ½ teaspoon baking soda
- 1 egg ½ teaspoon baking powder
- A pinch of salt

Directions:

1. In a bowl, mix butter with pumpkin puree and egg and blend well.

2. Add flaxseed meal, coconut flour, erythritol, baking soda, baking powder, nutmeg, cinnamon, and a pinch of salt and stir well.

3. Spoon this into a greased muffin pan, introduce in the oven at 350 degrees F and bake for 15 minutes.

4. Leave muffins to cool down and serve them as a snack.

5. Enjoy!

Nutrition:

- Calories: 65 kcal
- Protein: 2.82g
- Fat: 5.42g
- Carbohydrates: 2.27g
- Sodium: 57mg

Stuffed Avocado

Preparation Time: 10 minutes

Cooking Time: 0 minute

Servings: 2

Ingredients:

- 1 avocado, halved and pitted
- 10 ounces canned tuna, drained
- 2 tablespoons sun-dried tomatoes, chopped
- 1 and ½ tablespoon basil pesto
- 2 tablespoons black olives, pitted and chopped
- Salt and black pepper to the taste
- 2 teaspoons pine nuts, toasted and chopped
- 1 tablespoon basil, chopped

Directions:

1. In a bowl, combine the tuna with the sun-dried tomatoes and the rest of the ingredients except the avocado and stir.

2. Stuff the avocado halves with the tuna mix and serve as an appetizer.

Nutrition:

- Calories 233;
- Fat 9g;
- Fiber 3.5g;
- Carbs 11.4g;
- Protein 5.6g

Bulgur Lamb Meatballs

Preparation Time: 10 minutes

Cooking Time: 15 minutes

Servings: 6

Ingredients:

- 1 and ½ cups Greek yogurt
- ½ teaspoon cumin, ground
- 1 cup cucumber, shredded
- ½ teaspoon garlic, minced
- A pinch of salt and black pepper
- 1 cup bulgur
- 2 cups water
- 1-pound lamb, ground
- ¼ cup parsley, chopped
- ¼ cup shallots, chopped
- ½ teaspoon allspice, ground
- ½ teaspoon cinnamon powder
- 1 tablespoon olive oil

Directions:

1. In a bowl, combine the bulgur with the water, cover the bowl, leave aside for 10 minutes, drain and transfer to a bowl.

2. Add the meat, the yogurt and the rest of the ingredients except the oil, stir well and shape medium meatballs out of this mix.

3. Heat up a pan with the oil over medium-high heat, add the meatballs, cook them for 7 minutes on each side, arrange them all on a platter and serve as an appetizer.

Nutrition:

- Calories 300;
- Fat 9.6g;
- Fiber 4.6g;
- Carbs 22.6g;
- Protein 6.6g

Hummus with ground Lamb

Preparation Time: 10 minutes
Cooking Time: 15 minutes
Servings: 8
Ingredients:

- 10 ounces hummus
- 12 ounces lamb meat, ground
- ½ cup pomegranate seeds
- ¼ cup parsley, chopped
- 1 tablespoon olive oil
- Pita chips for serving

Directions:

1. Heat up a pan with the oil over medium-high heat, add the meat, and brown for 15 minutes stirring often.

2. Spread the hummus on a platter, spread the ground lamb all over, also spread the pomegranate seeds and the parsley and serve with pita chips as a snack.

Nutrition:

- Calories 133;
- Fat 9.7g;
- Fiber 1.7g;
- Carbs 6.4g;
- Protein 5

Creamy Spinach and Shallots Dip

Preparation Time: 10 minutes
Cooking Time: 0 minutes
 Servings: 4
Ingredients:

- 1 pound spinach, roughly chopped
- 2 shallots, chopped
- 2 tablespoons mint, chopped
- ¾ cup cream cheese, soft
- Salt and black pepper to the taste

Directions:

1. In a blender, combine the spinach with the shallots and the rest of the ingredients, and pulse well.

2. Divide into small bowls and serve as a party dip.

Nutrition:

- Calories 204;
- Fat 11.5g;
- Fiber 3.1g;
- Carbs 4.2g;
- Protein 5.9g

Cucumber Bites

Preparation Time: 10 minutes
Cooking Time: 0 minutes
Servings: 12
Ingredients:

- 1 English cucumber, sliced into 32 rounds
- 10 ounces hummus
- 16 cherry tomatoes, halved
- 1 tablespoon parsley, chopped
- 1-ounce feta cheese, crumbled

Directions:

1. Spread the hummus on each cucumber round, divide the tomato halves on each, sprinkle the cheese and parsley on to and serve as an appetizer.

Nutrition:

- Calories 162;
- Fat 3.4g;
- Fiber 2g;
- Carbs 6.4g;
- Protein 2.4g

Personal Pizza Biscuit

Preparation Time: 5 minutes
Cooking Time: 15 minutes
Servings: 1
Ingredients:

- 1 sachet Lean and Green select
- Buttermilk Cheddar Herb Biscuit.
- 2 tbsp. cold water
- Cooking spray
- 2 tbsp. no-sugar-added tomato sauce
- 1/4 cup reduced-fat shredded cheese

Directions:

1. Preheat oven to 350°F.

2. Mix biscuit and water, and spread mixture into a small, circular crust shape onto a greased, foil-lined baking sheet.

3. Bake for 10 minutes.

4. Top with tomato sauce and cheese, and cook till cheese is melted about 5 minutes.

Nutrition:

- Fats: 3.2g
- Cholesterol: 9.8mg
- Sodium: 10.5mg
- Protein: 3.6g

Cucumber Sandwich Bites

Preparation Time: 5 minutes

Cooking Time: 0 minutes

Servings: 12

Ingredients:

- 1 cucumber, sliced
- 8 slices whole wheat bread
- 2 tablespoons cream cheese, soft
- 1 tablespoon chives, chopped
- ¼ cup avocado, peeled, pitted and mashed
- 1 teaspoon mustard
- Salt and black pepper to the taste

Directions:

1. Spread the mashed avocado on each bread slice, also spread the rest of the ingredients except the cucumber slices.

2. Divide the cucumber slices on the bread slices, cut each slice in thirds, arrange on a platter and serve as an appetizer.

Nutrition:

- Calories 187;
- Fat 12.4g;
- Fiber 2.1g;
- Carbs 4.5g;
- Protein 8.2g

Sausage and Cheese Dip

Preparation Time: 10 minutes

Cooking Time: 130 minutes

Servings: 28

Ingredients:

- 8 ounces cream cheese
- A pinch of salt and black pepper
- 16 ounces sour cream
- 8 ounces pepper jack cheese, chopped
- 15 ounces canned tomatoes mixed with habaneros
- 1-pound Italian sausage, ground
- ¼ cup green onions, chopped

Directions:

1. Heat up a pan over medium heat, add sausage, stir and cook until it browns.

2. Add tomatoes mix, stir and cook for 4 minutes more.

3. Add a pinch of salt, pepper, and the green onions, stir and cook for 4 minutes.

4. Spread pepper jack cheese on the bottom of your slow cooker.

5. Add cream cheese, sausage mix, and sour cream, cover and cook on High for 2 hours.

6. Uncover your slow cooker, stir dip, transfer to a bowl, and serve.

7. Enjoy!

Nutrition:

- Calories: 132 kcal
- Protein: 6.79g
- Fat: 9.58g
- Carbohydrates: 6.22g
- Sodium: 362mg

Chicken Enchilada Bake

Preparation Time: 20 minutes

Cooking Time: 50 minutes

Servings: 5

Ingredients:

- 5 oz. Shredded chicken breast (boil and shred ahead) or 99 percent fat-free white chicken can be used in a pan.
- 1 can tomato paste
- 1 low sodium chicken broth can be fat-free
- 1/4 cup cheese with low fat mozzarella
- 1 tablespoon oil
- 1 tbsp. of salt
- Ground cumin, chili powder, garlic powder, oregano, and onion powder (all to taste)
- 1 to 2 zucchinis sliced long ways (similar to lasagna noodles) into thin lines
- Sliced (optional) olives

Directions:

1. Add olive oil in sauce pan over medium/high heat, stir in tomato paste and seasonings, and heat in chicken broth for 2-3 min.

2. Stirring regularly to boil, turn heat to low for 15 min.

3. Set aside and cool to ambient temperature.

4. Pull-strip of zucchini through enchilada sauce and lay flat on the pan's bottom in a small baking pan.

5. Next, add the chicken a little less than 1/4 cup of enchilada sauce and mix it.

6. Attach chicken to the cover ends to end of the baking tray.

7. Sprinkle some bacon over the chicken.

8. Add another layer of the pulled zucchini via enchilada sauce (similar to lasagna making).

9. When needed, cover with the remaining cheese and olives on top. Bake for 35 to 40 minutes.

10. Keep an eye on them.

11. When the cheese starts getting golden, cover with foil.

12. Serve and enjoy!

Nutrition:

- Calories: 312 Cal
- Carbohydrates: 21.3g
- Protein: 27g
- Fat: 10.2g

Tasty Onion and Cauliflower Dip

Preparation Time: 20 minutes

Cooking Time: 30 minutes

Servings: 24

Ingredients:

- 1 and ½ cups chicken stock
- 1 cauliflower head, florets separated
- ¼ cup mayonnaise
- ½ cup yellow onion, chopped
- ¾ cup cream cheese
- ½ teaspoon chili powder
- ½ teaspoon cumin, ground
- ½ teaspoon garlic powder
- Salt and black pepper to the taste

Directions:

1. Put the stock in a pot, add cauliflower and onion, heat up over medium heat, and cook for 30 minutes.

2. Add chili powder, salt, pepper, cumin, and garlic powder and stir.

3. Also, add cream cheese and stir a bit until it melts.

4. Blend using an immersion blender and mix with the mayo.

5. Transfer to a bowl and keep in the fridge for 2 hours before you serve it.

6. Enjoy!

Nutrition:

- Calories: 40 kcal
- Protein: 1.23g
- Fat: 3.31g
- Carbohydrates: 1.66g
- Sodium: 72mg

Chapter 13. Lunch Recipes

Polenta with Seared Pears

Preparation Time: 10 minutes
Cooking Time: 50 minutes
Servings: 1
Ingredients:

- One cup water, divided, plus more as needed
- 1/2 cups coarse cornmeal
- One tablespoon pure maple syrup
- 1/4 tablespoon molasses
- 1/4 teaspoon ground cinnamon
- 1/2 ripe pears, cored and diced
- 1/4 cup fresh cranberries
- 1/4 teaspoon chopped fresh rosemary leaves

Directions:

1. In a pan, cook 5 cups of water to a simmer.

2. While whisking continuously to avoid clumping, slowly pour in the cornmeal. Cook, often stirring with a heavy spoon, for 30 minutes. The polenta should be thick and creamy.

3. While the polenta cooks, in a saucepan over medium heat, stir together the maple syrup, molasses, the remaining 1/4 cup of water, and the cinnamon until combined.

4. Bring it to a simmer. Add the pears and cranberries. Cook for 10 minutes, occasionally stirring, until the pears are tender and start to brown.

5. Remove from the heat. Stir in the rosemary and let the mixture sit for 5 minutes. If it is too thick, add another 1/4 cup of water and return to the heat.

6. Top with the cranberry-pear mixture.

Nutrition:

- Calories: 282
- Fat: 2g
- Protein: 4g
- Carbohydrates: 65g
- Fiber: 12g

Family Fun Pizza

Preparation Time: 30 minutes
Cooking Time: 25 minutes
Servings: 16
Ingredients:

Pizza crust:

- Water, warm (1 cup)
- Salt (1/2 teaspoon)
- Flour, whole wheat (1 cup)
- Olive oil (2 tablespoons)
- Dry yeast, quick active (1 package)
- Flour, all purpose (1 ½ cups)
- Cornmeal
- Olive oil

Filling:

- Onion, chopped (1 cup)
- Mushrooms, sliced, drained (4 ounces)
- Garlic cloves, chopped finely (2 pieces)
- Parmesan cheese, grated (1/4 cup)
- Ground lamb, 80% lean (1 pound)
- Italian seasoning (1 teaspoon)
- Pizza sauce (8 ounces)
- Mozzarella cheese, shredded (2 cups)

Directions:

1. Mix yeast with warm water. Combine with flours, oil (2 tablespoons), and salt by stirring and then beating vigorously for half a minute. Let the dough sit for twenty minutes.

2. Preheat oven at 350 degrees Fahrenheit.

3. Prep 2 square pans (8-inch) by greasing with oil before sprinkling with cornmeal.

4. Cut the rested dough in half; place each half inside each pan. Set aside, covered, for thirty to forty-five minutes. Cook in the air fryer for twenty to twenty-two minutes.

5. Sauté the onion, beef, garlic, and Italian seasoning until beef is completely cooked. Drain and set aside.

6. Cover the air-fried crusts with pizza sauce before topping with beef mixture, cheeses, and mushrooms.

7. Return to oven and cook for twenty minutes.

Nutrition:

- Calories 215
- Fat 0g
- Protein 10g
- Carbohydrates 20.0g

Overnight Chocolate Chia Pudding

Preparation Time: 2 minutes
Cooking Time: overnight to chill
Servings: 1
Ingredients:

- 1/8 cup chia seeds
- 1/2 cup unsweetened nondairy milk

- One tablespoon raw cocoa powder
- 1/2 teaspoon vanilla extract
- 1/2 teaspoon pure maple syrup

Directions:

1. Stir together the chia seeds, milk, cacao powder, vanilla, and maple syrup in a large bowl.

2. Divide between two (1/2-pint) covered glass jars or containers.

3. Refrigerate overnight.

4. Stir before serving.

Nutrition:

- Calories: 213
- Fat: 10g
- Protein: 9g
- Carbohydrates: 20g
- Fiber: 15g

Bacon Wings

Preparation Time: 15 minutes

Cooking Time: 1 hour 15 minutes

Servings: 12

Ingredients:

- Bacon strips (12 pieces)
- Paprika (1 teaspoon)
- Black pepper (1 tablespoon)
- Oregano (1 teaspoon)
- Chicken wings (12 pieces)
- Kosher salt (1 tablespoon)
- Brown sugar (1 tablespoon)
- Chili powder (1 teaspoon)
- Celery sticks
- Blue cheese dressing

Directions:

1. Preheat the air fryer at 325 degrees Fahrenheit.

2. Mix sugar, salt, chili powder, oregano, pepper, and paprika. Coat chicken wings with this dry rub.

3. Wrap a bacon strip around each wing. Arrange wrapped wings in the air fryer basket.

4. Cook for thirty minutes on each side in the air fryer. Let cool for five minutes.

5. Serve and enjoy with celery and blue cheese.

Nutrition:

- Calories 100
- Fat 0g
- Protein 0g
- Carbohydrates 0g

Greek Style Mini Burger Pies

Preparation Time: 15 minutes

Cooking Time: 40 minutes

Servings: 6

Ingredients:

Burger mixture:

- Onion, large, chopped (1 piece)
- Red bell peppers, roasted, diced (1/2 cup)
- Ground lamb, 80% lean (1 pound)
- Red pepper flakes (1/4 teaspoon)
- Feta cheese, crumbled (2 ounces)

Baking mixture:

- Milk (1/2 cup)
- Biscuit mix, classic (1/2 cup)
- Eggs (2 pieces)

Directions:

1. Preheat oven at 350 degrees Fahrenheit.

2. Grease 12 muffin cups using cooking spray.

3. Cook the onion and beef in a skillet heated on medium-high. Once beef is browned and cooked through, drain and let cool for five minutes. Stir together with feta cheese, roasted red peppers, and red pepper flakes.

4. Whisk the baking mixture ingredients together. Fill each muffin cup with baking mixture (1 tablespoon).

5. Air-fry for twenty-five to thirty minutes. Let cool before serving.

Nutrition:

- Calories 270
- Fat 10g
- Protein 10g
- Carbohydrates 10g

Bacon Spaghetti Squash Carbonara

Preparation Time: 20 minutes

Cooking Time: 40 minutes

Servings: 4

Ingredients:

- 1 small spaghetti squash
- 6 ounces' bacon (roughly chopped)
- 1 large tomato (sliced)
- 2 chives (chopped)
- 1garlic clove (minced)
- 6 ounces low-fat cottage cheese
- 1 cup gouda cheese (grated)
- 2 tablespoons olive oil
- Salt and pepper, to taste

Directions:

1. Preheat the oven to 350°F.

2. Cut the squash spaghetti in half, brush with some olive oil and bake for 20–30 minutes, skin side up. Remove from the oven and remove the core with a fork, creating the spaghetti.

3. Heat one tablespoon of olive oil in a skillet. Cook the bacon for about 1 minute until crispy.

4. Quickly wipe out the pan with paper towels.

5. Heat another tablespoon of oil and sauté the garlic, tomato, and chives for 2–3 minutes. Add the spaghetti and sauté for another 5 minutes, occasionally stirring to keep from burning.

6. Begin to add the cottage cheese, about two tablespoons at a time. If the sauce becomes thick, add about a cup of water. The sauce should be creamy but not too runny or thick. Allow cooking for another 3 minutes.

7. Serve immediately.

Nutrition:

*   Calories: 305
*   Total Fat: 21g
*   Net Carbs: 8g
*   Protein: 18g

Slow Cooker Savory Butternut Squash Oatmeal

Preparation Time: 15 minutes

Cooking Time: 6 to 8 hours

Servings: 1

Ingredients:

*   1/4 cup steel-cut oats
*   1/2 cups cubed (1/2-inch pieces), peeled butternut squash (freeze any leftovers after preparing a whole squash for future meals)
*   3/4 cups of water
*   1/16 cup unsweetened nondairy milk
*   1/4 tablespoon chia seeds
*   1/2 teaspoons yellow miso paste
*   3/4 teaspoons ground ginger
*   1/4 tablespoon sesame seeds, toasted
*   1/4 tablespoon chopped scallion, green parts only
*   Shredded carrot, for serving (optional)

Directions:

1. In a slow cooker, combine the oats, butternut squash, and water.

2. Cover the slow cooker and cook on low for 6 to 8 hours, or until the squash is fork-tender.

3. Using a potato masher or heavy spoon, roughly mash the cooked butternut squash.

4. Stir to combine with the oats.

5. Whisk together the milk, chia seeds, miso paste, and ginger in a large bowl. Stir the mixture into the oats.

6. Top your oatmeal bowl with sesame seeds and scallion for more plant-based fiber, top with shredded carrot (if using).

Nutrition:

*   Calories: 230
*   Fat: 5g
*   Protein: 7g
*   Carbohydrates: 40g
*   Fiber: 9g

Spiced Sorghum and Berries

Preparation Time: 5 minutes

Cooking Time: 1 hour

Servings: 1

Ingredients:

*   1/4 cup whole-grain sorghum
*   1/4 teaspoon ground cinnamon
*   1/4 teaspoon Chinese five-spice powder
*   3/4 cups water
*   1/4 cup unsweetened nondairy milk
*   1/4 teaspoon vanilla extract
*   1/2 tablespoons pure maple syrup
*   1/2 tablespoon chia seed
*   1/8 cup sliced almonds
*   1/2 cups fresh raspberries, divided

Directions:

1. Using a large pot over medium-high heat, stir together the sorghum, cinnamon, five-spice powder, and water.

2. Wait for the water to a boil, cover it, and reduce the heat to medium-low.

3. Cook for one hour, or until the sorghum is soft and chewy. If the sorghum grains are still hard, add another cup of water and cook for 15 minutes more.

4. Using a glass measuring cup, whisk together the milk, vanilla, and maple syrup to blend.

5. Add the mixture to the sorghum and the chia seeds, almonds, and one cup of raspberries. Gently stir to combine.

6. When serving, top with the remaining one cup of fresh raspberries.

Nutrition:

*   Calories: 289

- Fat: 8g
- Protein: 9g
- Carbohydrates: 52g
- Fiber: 10g

Tropical Greens Smoothie

Preparation Time: 5 Minutes
Cooking Time: 0 Minutes
Servings: 1
Ingredients:

- One banana
- 1/2 large navel orange, peeled and segmented
- 1/2 cup frozen mango chunks
- 1 cup frozen spinach
- One celery stalk, broken into pieces
- One tablespoon cashew butter or almond butter
- 1/2 tablespoon spiraling
- 1/2 tablespoon ground flaxseed
- 1/2 cup unsweetened nondairy milk
- Water, for thinning (optional)

Directions:

1. In a high-speed blender or food processor, combine the bananas, orange, mango, spinach, celery, cashew butter, spiraling (if using), flaxseed, and milk.

2. Blend until creamy, adding more milk or water to thin the smoothie if too thick. Serve immediately—it is best served fresh.

Nutrition:

- Calories: 391
- Fat: 12g
- Protein: 13g
- Carbohydrates: 68g
- Fiber: 13g

Carrot Cake Oatmeal

Preparation Time: 10 minutes
Cooking Time: 15 minutes
Servings: 1
Ingredients:

- 1/8 cup pecans
- 1/2 cup finely shredded carrot
- 1/4 cup old-fashioned oats
- 5/8 cups unsweetened nondairy milk
- 1/2 tablespoon pure maple syrup
- 1/2 teaspoon ground cinnamon
- 1/2 teaspoon ground ginger
- 1/8 teaspoon ground nutmeg
- One tablespoon chia seed

Directions:

1. Over medium-high heat in a skillet, toast the pecans for 3 to 4 minutes, often stirring, until browned and fragrant (watch closely, as they can burn quickly).

2. Pour the pecans onto a cutting board and coarsely chop them. Set aside.

3. In an 8-quart pot over medium-high heat, combine the carrot, oats, milk, maple syrup, cinnamon, ginger, and nutmeg.

4. When it is already boiling, reduce the heat to medium-low.

5. Cook, uncovered, for 10 minutes, stirring occasionally.

6. Stir in the chopped pecans and chia seeds. Serve immediately.

Nutrition:

- Calories: 307
- Fat: 17g
- Protein: 7g
- Carbohydrates: 35g
- Fiber: 11g

Stewed Herbed Fruit

Preparation Time: 15 minutes
Cooking Time: 6 to 8 hours
Servings: 12
Ingredients:

- 2 cups dried apricots
- 2 cups prunes
- 2 cups dried unsulphured pears
- 2 cups dried apples
- 1 cup dried cranberries
- 1/4 cup honey
- 6 cups water
- 1 teaspoon dried thyme leaves
- 1 teaspoon dried basil leaves

Directions:

1. In a 6-quart slow cooker, mix all of the ingredients.

2. Cover and cook on low for 6 to 8 hours, or until the fruits have absorbed the liquid and are tender.

3. Store in the refrigerator for up to 1 week.

4. You can freeze the fruit in 1-cup portions for more extended storage.

Nutrition:

- Calories: 242 Cal
- Carbohydrates: 61g

- Sugar: 43g
- Fiber: 9g
- Fat: 0g
- Saturated Fat: 0g
- Protein: 2g
- Sodium: 11mg

Yogurt Garlic Chicken

Preparation Time: 30 minutes

Cooking Time: 60 min

Servings: 6

Ingredients:

- Pita bread rounds, halved (6 pieces)
- English cucumber, sliced thinly, w/ each slice halved (1 cup)

Chicken & vegetables:

- Olive oil (3 tablespoons)
- Black pepper, freshly ground (1/2 teaspoon)
- Chicken thighs, skinless, boneless (20 ounces)
- Bell pepper, red, sliced into half-inch portions (1 piece)
- Garlic cloves, chopped finely (4 pieces)
- Cumin, ground (1/2 teaspoon)
- Red onion, medium, sliced into half-inch wedges (1 piece)
- Yogurt, plain, fat free (1/2 cup)
- Lemon juice (2 tablespoons)
- Salt (1 ½ teaspoons)
- Red pepper flakes, crushed (1/2 teaspoon)
- Allspice, ground (1/2 teaspoon)
- Bell pepper, yellow, sliced into half-inch portions (1 piece)

Yogurt sauce:

- Olive oil (2 tablespoons)
- Salt (1/4 teaspoon)
- Parsley, flat leaf, chopped finely (1 tablespoon)
- Yogurt, plain, fat free (1 cup)
- Lemon juice, fresh (1 tablespoon)
- Garlic clove, chopped finely (1 piece)

Directions:

1. Mix the yogurt (1/2 cup), garlic cloves (4 pieces), olive oil (1 tablespoon), salt (1 teaspoon), lemon juice (2 tablespoons), pepper (1/4 teaspoon), allspice, cumin, and pepper flakes. Stir in the chicken and coat well. Cover and marinate in the fridge for two hours.

2. Preheat the air fryer at 400 degrees Fahrenheit.

3. Grease a rimmed baking sheet (18x13-inch) with cooking spray.

4. Toss the bell peppers and onion with remaining olive oil (2 tablespoons), pepper (1/4 teaspoon), and salt (1/2 teaspoon).

5. Arrange veggies on the baking sheets left side and the marinated chicken thighs (drain first) on the right side. Cook in the air fryer for twenty-five to thirty minutes.

6. Mix the yogurt sauce ingredients.

7. Slice air-fried chicken into half-inch strips.

8. Top each pita round with chicken strips, roasted veggies, cucumbers, and yogurt sauce.

Nutrition:

- Calories 380
- Fat 10g
- Protein 20g
- Carbohydrates 30g

Lemony Parmesan Salmon

Preparation Time: 10 minutes

Cooking Time: 25 minutes

Servings: 4

Ingredients:

- Butter, melted (2 tablespoons)
- Green onions, sliced thinly (2 tablespoons)
- Breadcrumbs, white, fresh (3/4 cup)
- Thyme leaves, dried (1/4 teaspoon)
- Salmon fillet, 1 ¼-pound (1 piece)
- Salt (1/4 teaspoon)
- Parmesan cheese, grated (1/4 cup)
- Lemon peel, grated (2 teaspoons)

Directions:

1. Preheat the oven at 350 degrees Fahrenheit.

2. Mist cooking spray onto a baking pan (shallow). Fill with pat-dried salmon. Brush salmon with butter (1 tablespoon) before sprinkling with salt.

3. Combine the breadcrumbs with onions, thyme, lemon peel, cheese, and remaining butter (1 tablespoon).

4. Cover salmon with the breadcrumb mixture. Air-fry for fifteen to twenty-five minutes.

Nutrition:

- Calories 290
- Fat 10g
- Protein 30g
- Carbohydrates 0g

Tuna Spinach Casserole

Preparation Time: 30 minutes
Cooking Time: 25 minutes
Servings: 8
Ingredients:

- Mushroom soup, creamy (18 ounces)
- Milk (1/2 cup)
- White tuna, solid, in-water, drained (12 ounces)
- Crescent dinner rolls, refrigerated (8 ounces)
- Egg noodles, wide, uncooked (8 ounces)
- Cheddar cheese, shredded (8 ounces)
- Spinach, chopped, frozen, thawed, drained (9 ounces)
- Lemon peel grated (2 teaspoons)

Directions:

1. Preheat the oven at 350 degrees Fahrenheit.
2. Mist cooking spray onto a glass baking dish (11x7-inch).
3. Follow package directions in cooking and draining the noodles.
4. Stir the cheese (1 ½ cups) and soup together in a skillet heated on medium. Once cheese melts, stir in your noodles, milk, spinach, tuna, and lemon peel. Once bubbling, pour into the prepped dish.
5. Unroll the dough and sprinkle with remaining cheese (1/2 cup). Roll up dough and pinch at the seams to seal. Slice into 8 portions and place over the tuna mixture.
6. Air-fry for twenty to twenty-five minutes.

Nutrition:

- Calories 400
- Fat 10g
- Protein 20g
- Carbohydrates 30g

Spiced Pumpkin Muffins

Preparation Time: 15 minutes
Cooking Time: 20 minutes
Servings: 1
Ingredients:

- 1/6 tablespoons ground flaxseed
- 1/24 cup of water
- 1/8 cups whole wheat flour
- 1/6 teaspoons baking powder
- 5/6 teaspoons ground cinnamon
- 1/12 teaspoon baking soda
- 1/12 teaspoon ground ginger
- 1/16 teaspoon ground nutmeg
- 1/32 teaspoon ground cloves
- 1/6 cup pumpkin puree
- 1/12 cup pure maple syrup
- 1/24 cup unsweetened applesauce
- 1/24 cup unsweetened nondairy milk
- 1/2 teaspoons vanilla extract

Directions:

1. Preheat the oven to 350°F. Line a 12-cup metal muffin pan with parchment paper liners or use a silicone muffin pan.
2. First, mix the flaxseed and water in a large bowl then keep it aside.
3. In a medium bowl, stir together the flour, baking powder, cinnamon, baking soda,ginger, nutmeg, and cloves.
4. In a medium bowl, stir up the maple syrup, pumpkin puree, applesauce, milk, and vanilla. Crease the wet ingredients into the dry ingredients making use of a spatula.
5. Fold the soaked flaxseed into the batter until evenly combined, but do not over mix the batter, or your muffins will become dense. Spoon about 1/4 cup of batter per muffin into your prepared muffin pan.
6. Bake for 18 to 20 minutes, or until a toothpick inserted into the center of a muffin comes out clean. Remove the muffins from the pan.
7. Transfer to a wire rack for cooling.
8. Store in an airtight container that is at room temperature.

Nutrition:

- Calories: 115
- Fat: 1g
- Protein: 3g
- Carbohydrates: 25g
- Fiber: 3g

Vanilla Buckwheat Porridge

Preparation Time: 5 minutes
Cooking Time: 25 minutes
Servings: 1
Ingredients:

- One cup of water
- 1/4 cup raw buckwheat grouts
- 1/4 teaspoon ground cinnamon
- 1/4 banana, sliced
- 1/16 cup golden raisins
- 1/16 cup dried currants
- 1/16 cup sunflower seeds
- 1/2 tablespoons chia seeds

1/4 tablespoon hemp seeds

1/4 tablespoon sesame seeds, toasted

1/8 cup unsweetened nondairy milk

1/4 tablespoon pure maple syrup

1/4 teaspoon vanilla extract

Directions:

1. Boil the water in a pot. Stir in the buckwheat, cinnamon, and banana.

2. Cook the mixture. Mix it and wait for it to boil, then reduce the heat to medium-low.

3. Cover the pot and cook for 15 minutes, or until the buckwheat is tender.

4. Remove from the heat.

5. Stir in the raisins, currants, sunflower seeds, chia seeds, hemp seeds, sesame seeds, milk, maple syrup, and vanilla. Cover the pot. Wait for 10 minutes before serving.

6. Serve as it is or top as desired.

Nutrition:

Calories: 353

Fat: 11g

Protein: 10g

Carbohydrates: 61g

Fiber: 10g

Raw-Cinnamon-Apple Nut Bowl

Preparation Time: 15 minutes

Cooking Time: 1 hour to chill

Servings: 1

Ingredients:

One green apple halved, seeded, and cored

3/4 Honeycrisp apples, halved, seeded, and cored

1/4 teaspoon freshly squeezed lemon juice

One pitted Medrol dates

1/8 teaspoon ground cinnamon

Pinch ground nutmeg

1/2 tablespoons chia seeds, plus more for serving (optional)

1/4 tablespoon hemp seed

1/8 cup chopped walnuts

Nut butter, for serving (optional)

Directions:

1. Finely dice half the green apple and one Honeycrisp apple. With the lemon juice, store it in an airtight container while you work on the next steps.

2. Coarsely chop the remaining apples and the dates. Transfer to a food processor and add the cinnamon and nutmeg.

3. Check it several times to see if it's mixing, then processes for 2 to 3 minutes to puree. Stir the puree into the reserved diced apples.

4. Stir in the chia seeds (if using), hemp seeds, and walnuts.

5. Chill for at least one hour.

6. Enjoy!

7. Serve as it is or top with additional chia seeds and nut butter (if using).

Nutrition:

- Calories: 274
- Fat: 8g
- Protein: 4g
- Carbohydrates: 52g
- Fiber: 9g

Mouthwatering Tuna Melts

Preparation Time: 15 minutes

Cooking Time: 20 minutes

Servings: 8

Ingredients:

- Salt (1/8 teaspoon)
- Onion, chopped (1/3 cup)
- Biscuits, refrigerated, flaky layers (16 1/3 ounces)
- Tuna, water packed, drained (10 ounces)
- Mayonnaise (1/3 cup)
- Pepper (1/8 teaspoon)
- Cheddar cheese, shredded (4 ounces)
- Tomato, chopped
- Sour cream
- Lettuce, shredded

Directions:

1. Preheat the air fryer at 325 degrees Fahrenheit.

2. Mist cooking spray onto a cookie sheet.

3. Mix tuna with mayonnaise, pepper, salt, and onion.

4. Separate dough so you have 8 biscuits; press each into 5-inch rounds.

5. Arrange 4 biscuit rounds on the sheet. Fill at the center with tuna mixture before topping with cheese. Cover with the remaining biscuit rounds and press to seal.

6. Air-fry for fifteen to twenty minutes. Slice each sandwich into halves. Serve each piece topped with lettuce, tomato, and sour cream.

Nutrition:

- Calories 320
- Fat 10g

* Protein 10g
* Carbohydrates 20g

Pepper Pesto Lamb

Preparation Time: 15 minutes
Cooking Time: 1 hour 15 minutes
Servings: 12
Ingredients:
Pesto:
* Rosemary leaves, fresh (1/4 cup)
* Garlic cloves (3 pieces)
* Parsley, fresh, packed firmly (3/4 cup)
* Mint leaves, fresh (1/4 cup)
* Olive oil (2 tablespoons)
Lamb:
* Red bell peppers, roasted, drained (7 ½ ounces)
* Leg of lamb, boneless, rolled (5 pounds)
* Seasoning, lemon pepper (2 teaspoons)

Directions:
1.   Preheat the oven at 325 degrees Fahrenheit.
2.   Mix the pesto ingredients in the food processor.
3.   Unroll the lamb and cover the cut side with pesto. Top with roasted peppers before rolling up the lamb and tying with kitchen twine.
4.   Coat lamb with seasoning (lemon pepper) and air-fry for one hour.

Nutrition:
* Calories 310
* Fat 10g
* Protein 40.0g
* Carbohydrates 0g

Peanut Butter and Cacao Breakfast Quinoa

Preparation Time: 5 Minutes
Cooking Time: 10 Minutes
Servings: 1
Ingredients:
* 1/3 cup quinoa flakes
* 1/2 cup unsweetened nondairy milk,
* 1/2 cup of water
* 1/8 cup raw cacao powder
* One tablespoon natural creamy peanut butter
* 1/8 teaspoon ground cinnamon
* One banana, mashed
* Fresh berries of choice, for serving
* Chopped nuts of choice, for serving

Directions:
1.   Using an 8-quart pot over medium-high heat, stir together the quinoa flakes, milk, water, cacao powder, peanut butter, and cinnamon.
2.   Cook and stir it until the mixture begins to simmer. Turn the heat to medium-low and cook for 3 to 5 minutes, stirring frequently.
3.   Stir in the bananas and cook until hot.
4.   Serve topped with fresh berries, nuts, and a splash of milk.

Nutrition:
* Calories: 471
* Fat: 16g
* Protein: 18g
* Carbohydrates: 69g
* Fiber: 16g

Best Whole Wheat Pancakes

Preparation Time: 10 minutes
Cooking Time: 20 minutes
Servings: 1
Ingredients:
* 3/4 tablespoons ground flaxseed
* Two tablespoons warm water
* 1/2 cups whole wheat pastry flour
* 1/8 cup rye flour
* 1/2 tablespoons double-acting baking powder
* 1/4 teaspoon ground cinnamon
* 1/8 teaspoon ground ginger
* One cup unsweetened nondairy milk
* 3/4 tablespoons pure maple syrup
* 1/4 teaspoon vanilla extract

Directions:
1.   Mix the warm water and flaxseed in a large bowl. Set aside for at least 5 minutes.
2.   Whisk together the pastry and rye flours, baking powder, cinnamon, and ginger.
3.   Whisk together the milk, maple syrup, and vanilla in a large bowl. Make use of a spatula, fold the wet ingredients into the dry ingredients. Fold in the soaked flaxseed until fully incorporated.
4.   Heat a large skillet or nonstick griddle over medium-high heat.
5.   Working in batches, three to four pancakes at a time, add 1/4-cup portions of batter to the hot skillet.
6.   Until golden brown, cook for 3 to 4 minutes each side or no liquid batter is visible.

Nutrition:
* Calories: 301

- Fat: 4g
- Protein: 10g
- Carbohydrates: 57g
- Fiber: 10g

Deliciously Homemade Pork Buns

Preparation Time: 20 minutes
Cooking Time: 25 minutes
Servings: 8
Ingredients:

- Green onions, sliced thinly (3 pieces)
- Egg, beaten (1 piece)
- Pulled pork, diced, w/ barbecue sauce (1 cup)
- Buttermilk biscuits, refrigerated (16 1/3 ounces)
- Soy sauce (1 teaspoon)

Directions:

1. Preheat the air fryer at 325 degrees Fahrenheit.
2. Use parchment paper to line your baking sheet.
3. Combine pork with green onions.
4. Separate and press the dough to form 8 four-inch rounds.
5. Fill each biscuit round's center with two tablespoons of pork mixture. Cover with the dough edges and seal by pinching. Arrange the buns on the sheet and brush with a mixture of soy sauce and egg.
6. Cook in the air fryer for twenty to twenty-five minutes.

Nutrition:

- Calories 240
- Fat 0g
- Protein 0g
- Carbohydrates 20g

Easiest Tuna Cobbler Ever

Preparation Time: 15 minutes
Cooking Time: 25 minutes
Servings: 4
Ingredients:

- Water, cold (1/3 cup)
- Tuna, canned, drained (10 ounces)
- Sweet pickle relish (2 tablespoons)
- Mixed vegetables, frozen (1 ½ cups)
- Soup, cream of chicken, condensed (10 ¾ ounces)
- Pimientos, sliced, drained (2 ounces)
- Lemon juice (1 teaspoon)
- Paprika

Directions:

1. Preheat the air fryer at 375 degrees Fahrenheit.
2. Mist cooking spray into a round casserole (1 ½ quarts).
3. Mix the frozen vegetables with milk, soup, lemon juice, relish, pimientos, and tuna in a saucepan. Cook for 8 minutes over medium heat.
4. Fill the casserole with the tuna mixture.
5. Mix the biscuit mix with cold water to form a soft dough. Beat for half a minute before dropping by four spoonsful into the casserole.
6. Dust the dish with paprika before air-frying for twenty to twenty-five minutes.

Nutrition:

- Calories 320
- Fat 10g
- Protein 20g
- Carbohydrates 30g

Vitamin C Smoothie Cubes

Preparation Time: 5 minutes
Cooking Time: 8 hours to chill
Servings: 1
Ingredients:

- 1/8 large papaya
- 1/8 mango
- 1/4 cups chopped pineapple, fresh or frozen
- 1/8 cup raw cauliflower florets, fresh or frozen
- 1/4 large navel oranges, peeled and halved
- 1/4 large orange bell pepper stemmed, seeded, and coarsely chopped

Directions:

1. Halve the papaya and mango, remove the pits, and scoop their soft flesh into a high-speed blender.
2. Add the pineapple, cauliflower, oranges, and bell pepper. Blend until smooth.
3. Evenly divide the puree between 2 (16-compartment) ice cube trays and place them on a level surface in your freezer. Freeze for at least 8 hours.
4. The cubes can be left in the ice cube trays until use or transferred to a freezer bag. The frozen cubes are good for about three weeks in a standard freezer, or up to 6 months in a chest freezer.

Nutrition:

- Calories: 96
- Fat: 1g
- Protein: 2g
- Carbohydrates: 24g
- Fiber: 4g

Chapter 14. Dinner Recipes

Tomato Fish Bake

Preparation Time: 5 minutes
Cooking Time: 30 minutes
Servings: 4
Ingredients:

- 4 cod fillets
- 4 tomatoes, sliced
- 4garlic cloves, minced
- 1 shallot, sliced
- 1 celery stalk, sliced
- 1 teaspoon fennel seeds
- 1 cup vegetable stock
- Salt and pepper to taste

Directions:

1. Layer the cod fillets and tomatoes in a deep-dish baking pan.
2. Add the rest of the ingredients and add salt and pepper.
3. Cook in the preheated oven at 350F for 20 minutes.
4. Serve the dish warm or chilled.

Nutrition:

- Calories: 299
- Fat: 3g
- Protein: 64g
- Carbohydrates: 2g

Broccoli Parmesan Pasta

Preparation Time: 10 minutes
Cooking Time: 10 minutes
Servings: 2
Ingredients:

- ounces broccoli florets
- tablespoons olive oil
- 2 tablespoons grated parmesan cheese
- 2 ounces rotini pasta, boiled
- ounces spaghetti, boiled
- Extra:
- 1/3 teaspoon salt
- ¼ teaspoon ground black pepper

Directions:

1. Chop broccoli florets into small pieces, place in a heatproof bowl, cover with a plastic wrap, and then microwave for 3 to 5 minutes until tender.

2. Drain broccoli well to remove all the moisture and then set aside until required.
3. Meanwhile, take a medium pot half full with water, place it over medium-high heat, bring the water to a boil, then add pasta and spaghetti and cook for 5 to 8 minutes until tender.
4. Drain the pasta, return it into the pot, add broccoli and cheese, and then stir in salt and black pepper until combined.

Nutrition:

- 353 Cal
- 10g Fats
- 9.7g Protein
- 34g Carb
- 5.4g Fiber

Marinated Chicken Breasts

Preparation Time: 5 minutes
Cooking Time: 2 hours
Servings: 4
Ingredients:

- 4 chicken breasts
- Salt and pepper to taste
- 1 lemon, juiced
- 1 rosemary sprig
- 1 thyme sprig
- 2garlic cloves, crushed
- 2 sage leaves
- 3 tablespoons extra virgin olive oil
- ½ cup buttermilk

Directions:

1. 1. Boil the chicken with salt and pepper and place it in a resealable bag.
2. 2. Add remaining ingredients and seal bag.
3. 3. Refrigerate for at least 1 hour.
4. 4. After 1 hour, heat a roasting pan over medium heat, then place the chicken on the grill.
5. 5. Cook on each side for 8-10 minutes or until juices are gone.
6. Serve the chicken warm with your favorite side dish.

Nutrition:

- Calories: 371
- Fat: 21g
- Protein: 46g
- Carbohydrates: 2g

Wild Rice Prawn Salad

Preparation Time: 5 minutes
Cooking Time: 35 minutes
Servings: 6
Ingredients:

- ¾ cup wild rice
- 1¾ cups chicken stock
- 1-pound prawns
- Salt and pepper to taste
- 2 tablespoons lemon juice
- 2 tablespoons extra virgin olive oil
- 2 cups arugula

Directions:

1. Combine the rice and chicken stock in a saucepan and cook until the liquid has been absorbed entirely.
2. Transfer the rice in a salad bowl.
3. Season the prawns with salt and pepper and drizzle them with lemon juice and oil.
4. Heat a grill pan over medium flame.
5. Place the prawns on the hot pan and cook on each side for 2-3 minutes.
6. For the salad, combine the rice with arugula and prawns and mix well.
7. Serve the salad fresh.

Nutrition:

- Calories: 207
- Fat: 4g
- Protein: 20.6g
- Carbohydrates: 17g

Chicken Cacciatore

Preparation Time: 5 minutes
Cooking Time: 45 minutes
Servings: 6
Ingredients:

- 2 tablespoons extra virgin olive oil
- 6 chicken thighs
- 1 sweet onion, chopped
- 2 garlic cloves, minced
- 2 red bell peppers, cored and diced
- 2 carrots, diced
- 1 rosemary sprig
- 1 thyme sprig
- 4 tomatoes, peeled and diced
- ½ cup tomato juice
- ¼ cup dry white wine
- 1 cup chicken stock
- 1 bay leaf
- Salt and pepper to taste

Directions:

1. Heat the oil in a heavy saucepan.
2. Cook chicken on all sides until golden.
3. Stir in the onion and garlic and cook for 2 minutes.
4. Stir in the rest of the ingredients and season with salt and pepper.
5. Cook on low heat for 30 minutes.
6. Serve the chicken cacciatore warm and fresh.

Nutrition:

- Calories: 363
- Fat: 14g
- Protein: 42g
- Carbohydrates: 9g

Curry and Sriracha Roasted Cauliflower

Preparation Time: 5 minutes
Cooking Time: 25 minutes
Servings: 2
Ingredients:

- ounces cauliflower florets
- 1/3 teaspoon salt
- 1 tablespoon curry powder
- 1 tablespoon Sriracha sauce
- 1 tablespoon olive oil

Directions:

1. Switch on the oven, then set it to 425 degrees F and let it preheat.
2. Meanwhile, take a medium bowl, place cauliflower in it, drizzle with Sriracha sauce and oil, and then season with salt and curry powder.
3. Toss the cauliflower florets until well coated and then arrange them in a single layer on a parchment-lined baking sheet.
4. Bake cauliflower for 20 to 25 minutes until tender and golden brown, stirring halfway.

Nutrition:

- 173 Cal
- 13.3g Fats
- 4.3g Protein
- 9.1g Carb
- 5.3g Fiber

Greek Roasted Fish

Preparation Time: 5 minutes
Cooking Time: 30 minutes
Servings: 4
Ingredients:

- 4 salmon fillets
- 1 tablespoon chopped oregano
- 1 teaspoon dried basil
- 1 zucchini, sliced
- 1 red onion, sliced
- 1 carrot, sliced
- 1 lemon, sliced
- 2 tablespoons extra virgin olive oil
- Salt and pepper to taste

Directions:

1. Add all the ingredients in a deep-dish baking pan.
2. Season with salt and pepper and cook in the preheated oven at 350F for 20 minutes.
3. Serve the fish and vegetables warm.

Nutrition:

- Calories: 328
- Fat: 13g
- Protein: 38g
- Carbohydrates: 8g

Fennel Wild Rice Risotto

Preparation Time: 5 minutes
Cooking Time: 35 minutes
Servings: 6
Ingredients:

- 2 tablespoons extra virgin olive oil
- 1 shallot, chopped
- 2garlic cloves, minced
- 1 fennel bulb, chopped
- 1 cup wild rice
- ¼ cup dry white wine
- 2 cups chicken stock
- 1 teaspoon grated orange zest
- Salt and pepper to taste

Directions:

1. Heat the oil in a heavy saucepan.
2. Add the garlic, shallot and fennel and cook for a few minutes until softened.
3. Stir in the rice and cook for 2 additional minutes then add the wine, stock and orange zest, with salt and pepper to taste.
4. Cook on low heat for 20 minutes.

5. Serve the risotto warm and fresh.

Nutrition:

- Calories: 162
- Fat: 2g
- Protein: 8g
- Carbohydrates: 20g

Zucchini Salmon Salad

Preparation Time: 5 minutes
Cooking Time: 10 minutes
Servings: 3
Ingredients:

- 2 salmon fillets
- 2 tablespoons soy sauce
- 2 zucchinis, sliced
- Salt and pepper to taste
- 2 tablespoons extra virgin olive oil
- 2 tablespoons sesame seeds
- Salt and pepper to taste

Directions:

1. Drizzle the salmon with soy sauce.
2. Heat a grill pan over medium flame. Cook salmon on the grill on each side for 2-3 minutes.
3. Season the zucchini with salt and pepper and place it on the grill as well. Cook on each side until golden.
4. Place the zucchini, salmon and the rest of the ingredients in a bowl.
5. Serve the salad fresh.

Nutrition:

- Calories: 224
- Fat: 19g
- Protein: 18g
- Carbohydrates: 0g

Seared Tofu in Soy Sauce and Black Pepper

Preparation Time: 35 minutes
Cooking Time: 8 minutes
Servings: 2
Ingredients:

- ounces tofu, ¼-inch thick sliced
- 1green onion, chopped
- tablespoons soy sauce
- ¼ teaspoon ground black pepper
- 1 teaspoon sesame seeds
- Extra:
- 1 tablespoon olive oil

Directions:

1.   Cut tofu into ¼-inch pieces, place them into a medium bowl and then add soy sauce and black pepper.

2.   Stir until coated and then let the tofu marinate for a minimum of 30 minutes.

3.   Then take a medium skillet pan, place it over medium-high heat, add oil and when hot, add tofu pieces and cook for 2 to 3 minutes per side until golden brown and crisp.

4.   When done, garnish tofu pieces with sesame seeds and onion and then serve.

Nutrition:

- 154 Cal
- 11g Fats
- 10g Protein
- 3g Carb
- 1g Fiber

Peanut Butter Mocha Smoothie

Preparation Time: 5 minutes

Cooking Time: 0 minutes

Servings: 2

Ingredients:

- ounces sliced pear
- tablespoons instant coffee powder
- 1 ½ cup almond milk, unsweetened

Directions:

1. Place all the ingredients in the order into a food processor or blender, and then pulse for 1 to 2 minutes until smooth.

2. Distribute smoothie between two glasses and then serve.

Nutrition:

- 117 Cal
- 3.6g Fats
- 1g Protein
- 20.1g Carb
- 2g Fiber

Warm Chorizo Chickpea Salad

Preparation Time: 5 minutes

Cooking Time: 20 minutes

Servings: 6

Ingredients:

- 1 tablespoon extra-virgin olive oil
- 4 chorizo links, sliced
- 1 red onion, sliced
- 4 roasted red bell peppers, chopped
- 1 can chickpeas, drained
- 2 cups cherry tomatoes
- 2 tablespoons balsamic vinegar
- Salt and pepper to taste

Directions:

1.   Heat the oil in a skillet and add the chorizo. Cook briefly just until fragrant then add the onion, bell peppers and chickpeas and cook for 2 additional minutes.

2.   Transfer the mixture in a salad bowl then add the tomatoes, vinegar, salt and pepper.

3.   Mix well and serve the salad right away.

Nutrition:

- Calories: 359
- Fat: 18g
- Protein: 15g
- Carbohydrates: 21g

Seafood Paella

Preparation Time: 5 minutes

Cooking Time: 45 minutes

Servings: 8

Ingredients:

- 2 tablespoons extra virgin olive oil
- 1 shallot, chopped
- 2garlic cloves, chopped
- 1 red bell pepper, cored and diced
- 1 carrot, diced
- 2 tomatoes, peeled and diced
- 1 cup wild rice
- 1 cup tomato juice
- 2 cups chicken stock
- 1 chicken breast, cubed
- Salt and pepper to taste
- 2 monkfish fillets, cubed
- ½ pound fresh shrimps, peeled and deveined
- ½ pound prawns
- 1 thyme sprig
- 1 rosemary sprig

Directions:

1.   Heat the oil in a skillet and stir in the shallot, garlic, bell pepper, carrot and tomatoes. Cook for a few minutes until softened.

2.   Stir in the rice, tomato juice, stock, chicken, salt and pepper and cook on low heat for 20 minutes.

3.   Add the rest of the ingredients and cook for 10 additional minutes.

4.   Serve the paella warm and fresh.

Nutrition:

- Calories: 245
- Fat: 8g
- Protein: 27g
- Carbohydrates: 20.6g

Mixed Fruit Parfait

Preparation Time: 5 minutes

Cooking Time: 0 minutes

Servings: 2

Ingredients:

- ounces of cherries mixed fruit
- tablespoons chia seeds
- ½ tablespoons shredded coconut, unsweetened
- tablespoons maple syrup
- ounces almond milk, unsweetened
- Extra:
- ½ teaspoon vanilla extract, unsweetened

Directions:

1 Take a medium bowl, place chia and coconut in it, add maple syrup and vanilla, pour in the milk and whisk until well combined.

2 Let the mixture rest for 30 minutes, then stir it and refrigerate for a minimum of 3 hours or overnight.

3 Assemble parfait and for this, divide half of the chia mixture into the bottom of serving glass, and then top evenly with three-fourth of mixed fruit.

4 Cover berries with remaining chia seed mixture and then place remaining mixed fruit on top.

Nutrition:

- 235 Cal
- 9.2g Fats
- 2.9g Protein
- 35.3g Carb

Herbed Roasted Chicken Breasts

Preparation Time: 5 minutes

Cooking Time: 50 minutes

Servings: 4

Ingredients:

- 2 tablespoons extra virgin olive oil
- 2 tablespoons chopped parsley
- 2 tablespoons chopped cilantro
- 1 teaspoon dried oregano
- 1 teaspoon dried basil
- 2 tablespoons lemon juice
- Salt and pepper to taste
- 4 chicken breasts

Directions:

1. Combine the oil, parsley, cilantro, oregano, basil, lemon juice, salt and pepper in a bowl.

2. Spread this mixture over the chicken and rub it well into the meat.

3. Place in a deep-dish baking pan and cover with aluminum foil.

4. Cook in the preheated oven at 350F for 20 minutes then remove the foil and cook for 25 additional minutes.

5. Serve the chicken warm and fresh with your favorite side dish.

Nutrition:

- Calories: 330
- Fat: 15g
- Protein: 40.7g
- Carbohydrates: 1g

Cherries Peanut Butter Smoothie

Preparation Time: 5 minutes

Cooking Time: 0 minutes

Servings: 2

Ingredients:

- ounces cherries
- 2 tablespoons peanut butter
- 1 ½ cup almond milk, unsweetened

Directions:

1 Place all the ingredients in the order into a food processor or blender, and then pulse for 1 to 2 minutes until smooth.

2 Distribute smoothie between two glasses and then serve.

Nutrition:

- 142 Cal
- 9.4g Fats
- 4.2g Protein
- 13g Carb
- 1.4g Fiber

Garlicky Tomato Chicken Casserole

Preparation Time: 5 minutes

Cooking Time: 50 minutes

Servings: 4

Ingredients:

- 4 chicken breasts
- 2 tomatoes, sliced
- 1 can diced tomatoes
- 2garlic cloves, chopped

1 shallot, chopped

1 bay leaf

1 thyme sprig

½ cup dry white wine

½ cup chicken stock

Salt and pepper to taste

Directions:

1. Combine the chicken and the remaining ingredients in a deep-dish baking pan.

2. Adjust the taste with salt and pepper and cover the pot with a lid or aluminum foil.

3. Cook in the preheated oven at 330F for 40 minutes.

4. Serve the casserole warm.

Nutrition:

Calories: 313

Fat: 8g

Protein: 47g

Carbohydrates: 6g

Chickpea Sandwich Filling

Preparation Time: 5 minutes

Cooking Time: 0 minutes

Servings: 2

Ingredients:

ounces chickpeas

1green onion, chopped

½ teaspoon dried dill

1 tablespoon mayonnaise

1 tablespoon lime juice

Extra:

¼ teaspoon salt

1/8 teaspoon ground black pepper

Directions:

1. Take a medium bowl, add chickpeas in it, and then add remaining ingredients.

2. Stir until well mixed and when ready, serve filling as a sandwich between two bread slices.

Nutrition:

356 Cal

7.5g Fats

11.6g Protein

60.6g Carb

7g Fiber

Cilantro and Lime Broccoli Rice

Preparation Time: 5 minutes

Cooking Time: 8 minutes

Servings: 2

Ingredients:

- ounces broccoli florets, finely chopped
- green onions, white and Green part separated
- tablespoons chopped cilantro
- ½ teaspoon garlic powder
- 1 teaspoon lime juice
- Extra:
- ¼ teaspoon cayenne pepper
- 1 tablespoon olive oil

Directions:

1 Take a medium skillet pan, place it over medium heat, add oil and when hot, add white parts of green onion and then cook for 1 to 2 minutes until softened.

2 Stir in garlic, add broccoli, stir until mixed, then cover the pan and cook for 4 to 5 minutes until broccoli has turned slightly soft.

3 Add lime juice and cilantro, sprinkle with cayenne pepper, and then cook for 30 seconds.

4 Taste to adjust seasoning and then serve.

Nutrition:

- 101 Cal
- 6.7g Fats
- 2g Protein
- 72g Carb
- 2g Fiber

Herbed Brown Rice

Preparation Time: 10 minutes

Cooking Time: 25 minutes

Servings: 2

Ingredients:

- 2/3 cup brown rice
- ¼ teaspoon salt
- 1 teaspoon Italian seasoning
- 1 tablespoon unsalted butter
- 1 ½ cup vegetable broth

Extra:

- 1/8 teaspoons ground black pepper

Directions:

1. Take a medium saucepan, place it over medium heat, add butter and when it melts, add rice, stir well, and then cook for 3 minutes.

2. Pour in broth, season with salt, black pepper, and Italian seasoning, stir until combined, and then bring the mixture to a boil.

3. Switch heat to medium-low heat, simmer rice for 20 to 25 minutes until rice has absorbed all the liquid and turned tender.

Nutrition:

- 136 Cal
- 3g Fats
- 3g Protein
- 24g Car
- 1g Fiber

Grilled Salmon with Pineapple Salsa

Preparation Time: 5 minutes

Cooking Time: 30 minutes

Servings: 4

Ingredients:

- 4 salmon fillets
- Salt and pepper to taste
- 2 tablespoons Cajun seasoning
- 1 fresh pineapple, peeled and diced
- 1 cup cherry tomatoes, quartered
- 2 tablespoons chopped cilantro
- 2 tablespoons chopped parsley
- 1 teaspoon dried mint
- 2 tablespoons lemon juice
- 2 tablespoons extra virgin olive oil
- 1 teaspoon honey
- Salt and pepper to taste

Directions:

1. Add salt, pepper and Cajun seasoning to the fish.

2. Heat a grill pan over medium flame. Cook fish on the grill on each side for 3-4 minutes.

3. For the salsa, mix the pineapple, tomatoes, cilantro, parsley, mint, lemon juice and honey in a bowl. Season with salt and pepper.

4. Serve the grilled salmon with the pineapple salsa.

Nutrition:

- Calories: 332
- Fat: 12g
- Protein: 34g
- Carbohydrates: 0g

Pan Fried Salmon

Preparation Time: 5 minutes

Cooking Time: 20 minutes

Servings: 4

Ingredients:

- 4 salmon fillets
- Salt and pepper to taste
- 1 teaspoon dried oregano
- 1 teaspoon dried basil
- 3 tablespoons extra virgin olive oil

Directions:

1. Season the fish with salt, pepper, oregano and basil.

2. Heat the oil in a pan and place the salmon in the hot oil, with the skin facing down.

3. Fry on each side for 2 minutes until golden brown and fragrant.

4. Serve the salmon warm and fresh.

Nutrition:

- Calories: 327
- Fat: 25g
- Protein: 36g
- Carbohydrates: 0.3g

Spicygarlic Pasta

Preparation Time: 5 minutes

Cooking Time: 5 minutes

Servings: 2

Ingredients:

- ounces fettuccine pasta, boiled
- 1 tablespoon minced garlic
- ½ teaspoon red chili flakes
- 1 teaspoon lime juice
- 1 ½ tablespoon olive oil

Directions:

1 Take a medium skillet pan, place it over medium heat, add oil and when hot, add garlic and then cook for 1 minute until golden.

2 Stir in chili flakes, cook for 20 seconds, then add pasta and toss to coat.

3 Drizzle lime juice over pasta, cook for 1 minute until hot, and then serve.

Nutrition:

- 490 Cal
- 11.4g Fats
- 13.5g Protein
- 83.3g Carb
- 4g Fiber

Chai Cardamom Vanilla Smoothie

Preparation Time: 5 minutes

Cooking Time: 0 minutes

Servings: 2

Ingredients:

- ½ teaspoon ground ginger
- ½ teaspoon ground cinnamon
- ½ teaspoon ground cloves
- ½ teaspoon ground cardamom
- 2 cups almond milk, unsweetened

Extra:

- ½ teaspoon ground nutmeg
- ½ teaspoon ground allspice

Directions:

1. Place all the ingredients in the order into a food processor or blender, and then pulse for 1 to 2 minutes until smooth.

2. Distribute smoothie between two glasses and then serve.

Nutrition:

- 92 Cal
- 5.7g Fats
- 2.3g Protein
- 7.8g Carb
- 0.5g Fiber

Mediterranean Chickpea Salad

Preparation Time: 5 minutes

Cooking Time: 20 minutes

Servings: 6

Ingredients:

- 1 can chickpeas, drained
- 1 fennel bulb, sliced
- 1 red onion, sliced
- 1 teaspoon dried basil
- 1 teaspoon dried oregano
- 2 tablespoons chopped parsley
- 4garlic cloves, minced
- 2 tablespoons lemon juice
- 2 tablespoons extra virgin olive oil
- Salt and pepper to taste

Directions:

1. Combine the chickpeas, fennel, red onion, herbs, garlic, lemon juice and oil in a salad bowl.

2. Add salt and pepper and serve the salad fresh.

Nutrition:

- Calories: 200
- Fat: 9g
- Protein: 4g
- Carbohydrates: 28g

Garlic Mashed Potatoes

Preparation Time: 5 minutes

Cooking Time: 10 minutes

Servings: 2

Ingredients:

- russet potatoes
- 1 clove of garlic
- 1 cup of water
- 1 tablespoon white miso paste
- 1/3 cup almond milk, unsweetened
- Extra:
- 1 1/3 teaspoon salt
- ¼ teaspoon black pepper

Directions:

1. Peel the potatoes, cut them into ½-inch rounds, and then place them into a medium pot.

2. Cover potatoes with water, add 1 teaspoon salt and garlic, place the pot over medium-high heat and bring to a boil.

3. Then switch heat to medium level and then cook potatoes for 10 to 15 minutes until tender.

4. When done, drain the potatoes, return them into the pot, and then add milk and mash well until smooth.

5. Stir in remaining salt and black pepper until mixed, add miso paste and whip the mixture by using an immersion blender until reach to desired consistency.

Nutrition:

- 274.5 Cal
- 0.6g Fats
- 5.5g Protein
- 61.8g Carb
- 12g Fiber

Chicken Broccoli Salad with Avocado Dressing

Preparation Time: 5 minutes

Cooking Time: 40 minutes

Servings: 6

Ingredients:

- 2 chicken breasts
- 1-pound broccoli, cut into florets
- 1 avocado, peeled and pitted
- ½ lemon, juiced
- 2garlic cloves

- ¼ teaspoon chili powder
- ¼ teaspoon cumin powder
- Salt and pepper to taste

Directions:

1. Cook the chicken in a large pot of salty water.
2. Drain and cut the chicken into small cubes. Place in a salad bowl.
3. Add the broccoli and mix well.
4. Combine the avocado, lemon juice, garlic, chili powder, cumin powder, salt and pepper in a blender. Pulse until smooth.
5. Spoon the dressing over the salad and mix well.
6. Serve the salad fresh.

Nutrition:

- Calories: 195
- Fat: 11g
- Protein: 14g
- Carbohydrates: 3g

Honeygarlic Butter Roasted Carrots

Preparation Time: 5 minutes
Cooking Time: 20 minutes
Servings: 2
Ingredients:

- carrots
- ½ tablespoon minced garlic
- 1/8 teaspoon salt
- 2/3 tablespoon honey
- 1 tablespoon chopped cilantro
- Extra:
- 1/8 teaspoon ground black pepper
- 1 2/3 tablespoon butter, unsalted

Directions:

1 Switch on the oven, then set it to 425 degrees F and let it preheat.

2 Meanwhile, prepare the carrot, and for this, peel them and diagonally cut them into 2-inch pieces.

3 Take a medium skillet pan, place it over medium heat, add butter and when it melts, add garlic and then cook for 1 minute until golden.

4 Remove pan from heat, add honey into the pan and then stir until well combined.

5 Add carrots into the pan, season with salt and black pepper and mix until well coated.

6 Arrange carrots in a single layer on a baking sheet greased with oil and then bake for 15 to 18 minutes until carrots have become tender and golden brown.

Nutrition:

- 143 Cal
- 9.5g Fats
- 0.7g Protein
- 14g Carb
- 21g Fiber

Cauliflower Rice Stuffed Peppers

Preparation Time: 10 minutes
Cooking Time: 25 minutes
Servings: 2
Ingredients:

- 1 red bell pepper
- 1green bell pepper
- ounces cauliflower florets
- 1green onion, chopped
- ounces white beans
- Extra:
- ½ teaspoon salt
- ¼ teaspoon ground black pepper
- ½ teaspoon red chili powder

Directions:

1 Switch on the oven, then set it to 375 degrees F and let it preheat.

2 Meanwhile, place the cauliflower florets into a food processor and then pulse for 1 minute until the mixture resembles rice.

3 Then take a medium skillet pan, place it over medium heat, add oil and when hot, add cauliflower rice, season with salt and black pepper, and then cook for 2 minutes, covering the pan.

4 Remove pan from heat, then add remaining ingredients except for red pepper and stir until mixed.

5 Prepare the pepper and for this, cut each pepper into half, remove the stem and seeds and then arrange them into a baking dish.

6 Stuff each pepper with cauliflower and black bean mixture, cover with the foil, and then bake for 15 minutes.

7 Uncover the baking dish, switch heat of the oven to 400 degrees F and then continue baking for 5 to 10 minutes until peppers have turned soft and the top has turned golden brown.

Nutrition:

- 207 Cal
- 5g Fats
- 9.3g Protein
- 35.1g Carb

10.4g Fiber

Black Bean and Brown Rice Bowl

Preparation Time: 5 minutes

Cooking Time: 10 minutes

Servings: 2

Ingredients:

ounces black beans

1 cup of brown rice

1 tablespoon olive oil

ounces tomato sauce

1 cup vegetable broth

Extra:

1/3 teaspoon salt

1 teaspoon red chili powder

Directions:

1 Take a medium skillet pan, place it over medium-high heat, add oil and when hot, add rice and stir in red chili powder.

2 Cook the rice for 2 minutes until nicely golden brown, add remaining ingredients and stir until combined.

3 Switch heat to medium-low level and cook rice for 10 to 15 minutes until rice has turned tender.

4 When done, remove the pan from heat, let the mixture for 5 minutes and then fluff with by using a fork.

Nutrition:

- 577 Cal
- 10.3g Fats
- 14.4g Protein
- 106.7g Carb

Coconut Fudge

Preparation Time: 20 minutes
Cooking Time: 60 minutes
Servings: 12
Ingredients:

- 2 cups coconut oil
- ½ cup dark cocoa powder
- ½ cup coconut cream
- ¼ cup almonds, chopped
- ¼ cup coconut, shredded
- 1 teaspoon almond extract
- Pinch of salt
- Stevia to taste

Directions:

1. Pour your coconut oil and coconut cream in a bowl, whisking with an electric beater until smooth. Once the mixture becomes smooth and glossy, do not continue.

2. Begin to add in your cocoa powder while mixing slowly, making sure that there aren't any lumps.

3. Add in the rest of your ingredients, and mix well.

4. Line a pan with parchment paper, and freeze until it sets.

5. Slice into squares before serving.

Nutrition:

- Calories: 172
- Fat: 20g
- Carbohydrates: 3g

Sweet Almond Bites

Preparation Time: 30 minutes
Cooking Time: 90 minutes
Servings: 12
Ingredients:

- 18 ounces butter, grass fed
- 2 ounces heavy cream
- ½ cup Stevia
- 2/3 cup cocoa powder
- 1 teaspoon vanilla extract, pure
- 4 tablespoons almond butter

Direction:

1. Use a double boiler to melt your butter before adding in all of your remaining ingredients.

2. Place the mixture into molds, freezing for two hours before serving.

Nutrition:

- Calories: 350
- Protein: 2g
- Fat: 38g

Baked Tuna with Asparagus

Preparation Time: 10 minutes
Cooking Time: 10 minutes
Servings: 2
Ingredients:

- 2 tuna steak
- 1 cup asparagus, trimmed
- 1 tsp. almond butter
- 1 tsp. rosemary
- 1/2 tsp. oregano
- 1/2 tsp. garlic powder
- 1tsp. lemon juice
- 1/2 tsp. ginger powder
- 1 tbsp. olive oil
- 1 tsp. red chili powder
- Salt and pepper to taste

Directions:

1. Marinate the tuna using oregano, lemon juice, salt, pepper, red chili powder, garlic, ginger, and let it sit for 10 minutes.

2. In a pan, add the olive oil.

3. Fry the tuna steaks 2 minutes per side.

4. In another pan, melt the almond butter.

5. Toss the asparagus with salt, pepper, and rosemary for 3 minutes.

6. Serve.

Nutrition:

- Fat: 4.7g
- Cholesterol: 0.0mg
- Sodium: 98.5mg
- Potassium: 171.6mg
- Carbohydrate: 3.2g

Chocolate Orange Bites

Preparation Time: 20 minutes
Cooking Time: 120 minutes
Servings: 6
Ingredients:

- 10 ounces coconut oil

- 4 tablespoons cocoa powder
- ¼ teaspoon orange extract
- Stevia to taste

Directions:

1. Melt half of your coconut oil using a double boiler, and then add in your stevia and orange extract.

2. Get out candy molds, pouring the mixture into it. Fill each mold halfway, and then place in the fridge until they set.

3. Melt the other half of your coconut oil, stirring in your cocoa powder and stevia, making sure that the mixture is smooth with no lumps.

4. Pour into your molds, filling them up all the way, and then allow it to set in the fridge before serving.

Nutrition:

- Calories: 188g
- Protein: 1g
- Fat: 21g
- Carbohydrates: 5g

Poached Pears

Preparation Time: 8 minutes

Cooking Time: 10 minutes

Servings: 2

Ingredients:

- 1 tbsp. lime juice
- 2 tsp. lime zest
- 1 cinnamon stick
- 2 whole pears, peeled
- 1 cup of water
- Fresh mint leaves for garnish

Directions:

1. Add all Ingredients except for the mint leaves to the Instant Pot.

2. Seal the Instant Pot and choose the MANUAL button.

3. Cook on HIGH for 10 minutes.

4. Perform a natural pressure release.

5. Remove the pears from the pot.

6. Serve in bowls and garnish with mint on top.

Nutrition:

- Calories: 59
- Fat: 0.1g
- Carbs: 14g
- Protein: 0.3g

Lamb Stuffed Avocado

Preparation Time: 10 minutes

Cooking Time: 40 minutes

Servings: 4

Ingredients:

- 2 avocados
- 1 1/2 cup minced lamb
- 1/2 cup cheddar cheese, grated
- 1/2 cup parmesan cheese, grated
- 2 tbsp. almond, chopped
- 1 tbsp. coriander, chopped
- 2 tbsp. olive oil
- 1 tomato, chopped
- 1 jalapeno, chopped
- Salt and pepper to taste
- 1 tsp. garlic, chopped
- 1-inchginger, chopped

Directions:

1. Cut the avocados in half. Remove the pit and scoop out some flesh to stuff it later.

2. In a skillet, add half of the oil.

3. Toss the ginger, garlic for 1 minute.

4. Add the lamb and toss for 3 minutes.

5. Add the tomato, coriander, parmesan, jalapeno, salt, pepper, and cook for 2 minutes.

6. Take off the heat. Stuff the avocados.

7. Sprinkle the almonds, cheddar cheese, and add olive oil on top.

8. Add to a baking sheet and bake for 30 minutes. Serve.

Nutrition:

- Fat: 19.5g
- Cholesterol: 167.5mg
- Sodium: 410.7mg
- Potassium: 617.1mg
- Carbohydrate: 13.1g

Nutmeg Nougat

Preparation Time: 30 minutes

Cooking Time: 60 minutes

Servings: 12

Ingredients:

- 1 cup heavy cream
- 1 cup cashew butter
- 1 cup coconut, shredded
- ½ teaspoon nutmeg
- 1 teaspoon vanilla extract, pure
- Stevia to taste

Directions:

1.   Melt your cashew butter using a double boiler, and then stir in your vanilla extract, dairy cream, nutmeg, and stevia. Make sure it's mixed well.

2.   Remove from heat, allowing it to cool down before refrigerating it for half an hour.

3.   Shape into balls, and coat with shredded coconut. Chill for at least two hours before serving.

Nutrition:

- Calories: 341
- Fat: 34g
- Carbohydrates: 5g

Strawberry Cheesecake Minis

Preparation Time: 30 minutes

Cooking Time: 120 minutes

Servings: 12

Ingredients:

- 1 cup coconut oil
- 1 cup coconut butter
- ½ cup strawberries, sliced
- ½ teaspoon lime juice
- 2 tablespoons cream cheese, full fat
- Stevia to taste

Directions:

1.   Blend your strawberries together.

2.   Soften your cream cheese, and then add in your coconut butter.

3.   Combine all ingredients together, and then pour your mixture into silicone molds.

4.   Freeze for at least two hours before serving.

Nutrition:

- Calories: 372
- Protein: 1g
- Fat: 41g
- Carbohydrates: 2g

Wine Figs

Preparation Time: 5 minutes

Cooking Time: 3 minutes

Servings: 2

Ingredients:

- ½ cup pine nuts
- 1 cup red wine
- 1 lb. figs
- Sugar, as needed

Directions:

1.   Slowly pour the wine and sugar into the Instant Pot.

2.   Arrange the trivet inside it; place the figs over it. Close the lid and lock. Ensure that you have sealed the valve to avoid leakage.

3.   Press MANUAL mode and set timer to 3 minutes.

4.   After the timer reads zero, press CANCEL and quick-release pressure.

5.   Carefully remove the lid.

6.   Divide figs into bowls, and drizzle wine from the pot over them.

7.   Top with pine nuts and enjoy.

Nutrition:

- Calories: 95
- Fat: 3g
- Carbs: 5g
- Protein: 2g

Cocoa Brownies

Preparation Time: 10 minutes

Cooking Time: 30 minutes

Servings: 12

Ingredients:

- 1 egg
- 2 tablespoons butter, grass-fed
- 2 teaspoons vanilla extract, pure
- ¼ teaspoon baking powder
- ¼ cup cocoa powder
- 1/3 cup heavy cream
- ¾ cup almond butter
- Pinch sea salt

Directions:

1.   Break your egg into a bowl, whisking until smooth.

2.   Add in all of your wet ingredients, mixing well.

3.   Mix all dry ingredients into a bowl.

4.   Sift your dry ingredients into your wet ingredients, mixing to form a batter.

5.   Get out a baking pan, greasing it before pouring in your mixture.

6.   Heat your oven to 350 and bake for twenty-five minutes.

7.   Allow it to cool before slicing and serve at room temperature or warm.

Nutrition:

- Calories: 184
- Protein: 1g
- Fat: 20g
- Carbohydrates: 1g

Mediterranean Chicken Salad

Preparation Time: 15 minutes

Cooking Time: 30 minutes

Servings: 4

Ingredients:

For Chicken:

1 3/4 lb. boneless, skinless chicken breast

1/4 teaspoon each of pepper and salt (or as desired)

1 1/2 tablespoon of butter, melted

For Mediterranean Salad:

1 cup of sliced cucumber

6 cups of romaine lettuce, that is torn or roughly chopped

10 pitted Kalamata olives

1 pint of cherry tomatoes

1/3 cup of reduced-fat feta cheese

1/4 teaspoon each of pepper and salt (or lesser)

1 small lemon juice (it should be about 2 tablespoons)

Directions:

1. Preheat your oven or grill to about 3500F.

2. Season the chicken with salt, butter, and black pepper

3. Roast or grill chicken until it reaches an internal temperature of 1650F in about 25 minutes.

4. Once your chicken breasts are cooked, remove and keep aside to rest for about 5 minutes before you slice it.

5. Combine all the salad ingredients you have and toss everything together very well.

6. Serve the chicken with a Mediterranean salad.

Nutrition:

Calories: 340 Cal

Protein: 45g

Carbohydrates: 9g

Fat: 14g

Baked Beef Zucchini

Preparation Time: 10 minutes

Cooking Time: 40 minutes

Servings: 4

Ingredients:

2 large zucchinis

1 cup minced beef

1 cup mushroom, chopped

1 tomato, chopped

1/2 cup spinach, chopped

- 1 tbsp. chives, minced
- 2 tbsp. olive oil
- Salt and pepper to taste
- 1 tbsp. almond butter
- 1 tsp. garlic powder
- 1 cup cheddar cheese, grated
- 1/3 tsp. ginger powder

Directions:

1. Preheat the oven to 400 degrees F.

2. Add aluminum foil on a baking sheet.

3. Cut the zucchini in half. Scoop out the seeds and make pockets to stuff it later.

4. In a pan, add the olive oil.

5. Toss the beef until brown.

6. Add the mushroom, tomato, chives, salt, pepper, garlic, ginger, and spinach.

7. Cook for 2 minutes. Take off the heat.

8. Stuff the zucchinis using the mix.

9. Add them onto the baking sheet. Sprinkle the cheese on top.

10. Add the butter on top. Bake for 30 minutes. Serve warm.

Nutrition:

- Fat: 12.8g
- Cholesterol: 79.7mg
- Sodium: 615.4mg
- Potassium: 925.8mg
- Carbohydrate: 26.8g

Easy Vanilla Bombs

Preparation Time: 20 minutes

Cooking Time: 45 minutes

Servings: 14

Ingredients:

- 1 cup macadamia nuts, unsalted
- ¼ cup coconut oil / ¼ cup butter
- 2 teaspoons vanilla extract, sugar-free
- 20 drops liquid Stevia
- 2 tablespoons erythritol, powdered

Directions:

1. Pulse your macadamia nuts in a blender, and then combine all of your ingredients together. Mix well.

2. Get out mini muffin tins with a tablespoon and a half of the mixture.

3. Refrigerate it for a half hour before serving.

Nutrition:

- Calories: 125
- Fat: 5g

- Carbohydrates: 5g

Chocolate Fondue

Preparation Time: 5 minutes
Cooking Time: 10 minutes
Servings: 2
Ingredients:

- 1 cup water
- ½ tsp. sugar
- ½ cup coconut cream
- ¾ cup dark chocolate, chopped

Directions:

1. Pour the water into your Instant Pot.
2. To a heatproof bowl, add the chocolate, sugar, and coconut cream.
3. Place in the Instant Pot.
4. Seal the lid, select MANUAL, and cook for 2 minutes. When ready, do a quick release and carefully open the lid. Stir well and serve immediately.

Nutrition:

- Calories: 216
- Fat: 17g
- Carbs: 11g
- Protein: 2g

Avocado Taco Boats

Preparation Time: 5 minutes
Cooking Time: 20 minutes
Servings: 4
Ingredients:

- 4grape tomatoes
- 2 large avocados
- 1 lbs. Ground beef
- 4 tablespoon taco seasoning
- 3/4 cup shredded sharp cheddar cheese
- 4 slices pickled jalapeño
- 1/4 cup salsa
- 3 shredded romaine leaves
- 1/4 cup sour cream
- 2/3 cup water

Directions:

1. Take a skillet of large size, grease it with oil, and heat it over medium-high heat. Cook the ground beef in it for 10-15 minutes or until it gives a brownish look.
2. Once the beef gets brown, drain the grease from the skillet and add the water and the taco seasoning.

3. Reduce the heat once the taco seasoning gets mixed well and simmer for 8-10 minutes.
4. Take both avocados and prepare their halves using a sharp knife.
5. Take each avocado shell and fill it with ¼ of the shredded romaine leaves.
6. Fill each shell with ¼ of the cooked ground beef.
7. Do the topping with sour cream, cheese, jalapeno, salsa, and tomato before you serve the delicious avocado taco boats.

Nutrition:

- Calories: 430
- Fat: 35g
- Carbohydrates: 5g
- Protein: 32g

Grandma's Rice

Preparation Time: 15 minutes
Cooking Time: 2 hours
Servings: 4
Ingredients:

- 40g butter
- 1/2 cup brown sugar
- 1/2 cup arborio rice
- 3 cups milk
- 1/2 tbsp. Ground cinnamon
- 1/8 tbsp. Ground nutmeg
- 1 tbsp. vanilla paste
- 1/2 cup raisins
- 300 ml. cream

Directions:

1. Preheat oven to 300F.
2. Grease a 1-liter ability oven-safe plate.
3. Heat butter in a saucepan and add sugar and rice.
4. Stir for 1 minute to thoroughly coat the rice.
5. Remove from heat and wish in milk, spices, and vanilla.
6. Stir through raisins then pour into prepared dish.
7. Bake for 30 minutes, then remove from the oven and stir well.
8. Drizzle over the cream and return to the oven for an additional hour.
9. Check that the rice is cooked through.
10. Return to the oven for 15-30 minutes if required.
11. Serve with extra cream and nutmeg.

Nutrition:

- Fat: 20g
- Protein: 23g
- Cholesterol: 25mg
- Carbohydrates: 30g
- Sodium: 1000mg

Jalapeno Lentil Burgers

Preparation Time: 15 minutes

Cooking Time: 10 minutes

Servings: 5

Ingredients:

- Dried red lentils; half cup; rinsed
- Chickpeas; 1 to 12 ounces can; rinsed
- Ground cumin; one teaspoon
- Chili powder; one teaspoon
- Sea salt; one teaspoon
- Packed cilantro; half cup
- Garlic cloves minced
- Jalapeno finely chopped
- Red onion; half, small; minced
- Red bell pepper
- Carrot; shredded
- Oat bran/oat flour; 1/4 cup (gluten-free)
- Lettuce/hamburger buns
  For Pico:
- Ripe mango (1) diced
- Ripe avocado (1) diced
- Red onion; half, small; finely diced
- Chopped cilantro; half cup
- Fresh lime juice; half teaspoon
- Sea salt

Directions:

1. Put all ingredients in a large bowl and mix.

2. Stir in the salt to compare.

3. Put a medium saucepan on medium heat, add lentils plus 1 1/2 cups of water, then bring water to a boil, cover it afterward, lower the heat to low, and then simmer lentils until the water is absorbed.

4. Drain, and set aside some extra water.

5. In a food processor, put the cooked lentils, chickpeas, garlic, sea salt, cilantro, chili powder and cumin, and blend until the beans and lentils are smooth.

6. Add tomato, red pepper, jalapeno, and carrot to compare.

7. Divide into 6 equal parts and use your hands to create dense patties.

8. Heat skillet over a medium-high flame; apply 1/2 tablespoon of olive oil

9. Place a few burgers in at a time and cook on either side for a couple of minutes, just until crisp and golden brown.

10. Repeat with remaining patties and add olive oil whenever desired.

11. Place the patties in a bun or lettuce and finish with mango avocado pico.

Nutrition:

- Carbohydrates: 34.9g
- Calories: 225 Cal
- Sugar: 7.7g
- Fats: 6.1g

Caramel Cones

Preparation Time: 25 minutes

Cooking Time: 120 minutes

Servings: 6

Ingredients:

- 2 tablespoons heavy whipping cream
- 2 tablespoons sour cream
- 1 tablespoon caramel sugar
- 1 teaspoon sea salt, fine
- 1/3 cup butter, grass-fed
- 1/3 cup coconut oil
- Stevia to taste

Directions:

1. Soften your coconut oil and butter, mixing together.

2. Mix all ingredients to form a batter, and then place them in molds.

3. Top with a little salt, and keep refrigerated until serving.

Nutrition:

- Calories: 100
- Fat: 12g
- Carbohydrates: 1g

Rhubarb Dessert

Preparation Time: 4 minutes

Cooking Time: 5 minutes

Servings: 2

Ingredients:

- 3 cups rhubarb, chopped
- 1 tbsp. ghee, melted
- 1/3 cup water
- 1 tbsp. stevia
- 1 tsp. vanilla extract

Directions:

1. Put all the listed Ingredients in your Instant Pot, cover, and cook on HIGH for 5 minutes.

2. Divide into small bowls and serve cold.

3. Enjoy!

Nutrition:

- Calories: 83
- Fat: 2g
- Carbs: 2g
- Protein: 2g

Rice Pudding

Preparation Time: 5 minutes

Cooking Time: 12 minutes

Servings: 2

Ingredients:

- ½ cup short grain rice
- ¼ cup of sugar
- 1 cinnamon stick
- 1½ cup milk
- 1 slice lemon peel
- Salt to taste

Directions:

1. Rinse the rice under cold water.

2. Put the milk, cinnamon stick, sugar, salt, and lemon peel inside the Instant Pot Pressure Cooker.

3. Close the lid, lock in place, and make sure to seal the valve. Press the PRESSURE button and cook for 10 minutes on HIGH.

4. When the timer beeps, choose the QUICK PRESSURE release. This will take about 2 minutes.

5. Remove the lid. Open the pressure cooker and discard the lemon peel and cinnamon stick. Spoon in a serving bowl and serve.

Nutrition:

- Calories: 111
- Fat: 6g
- Carbs: 21g
- Protein: 3g

Fluffy Bites

Preparation Time: 20 minutes

Cooking Time: 60 minutes

Servings: 12

Ingredients:

- 2 teaspoons cinnamon
- 2/3 cup sour cream
- 2 cups heavy cream
- 1 teaspoon scraped vanilla bean
- ¼ teaspoon cardamom

- 4 egg yolks
- Stevia to taste

Directions:

1. Start by whisking your egg yolks until creamy and smooth.

2. Get out a double boiler, and add your eggs with the rest of your ingredients. Mix well.

3. Remove from heat, allowing it to cool until it reaches room temperature.

4. Refrigerate for an hour before whisking well.

5. Pour into molds, and freeze for at least an hour before serving.

Nutrition:

- Calories: 363
- Protein: 2g
- Fat: 40g
- Carbohydrates: 1g

Apple Crisp

Preparation Time: 10 minutes

Cooking Time: 13 minutes

Servings: 2

Ingredients:

- 2 apples, sliced into chunks
- 1 tsp. cinnamon
- ¼ cup rolled oats
- 1/4 cup brown sugar
- ½ cup of water

Directions:

1. Put all the listed Ingredients in the pot and mix well.

2. Seal the pot, choose MANUAL mode, and cook at HIGH pressure for 8 minutes.

3. Release the pressure naturally and let sit for 5 minutes or until the sauce has thickened.

4. Serve and enjoy.

Nutrition:

- Calories: 218
- Fat: 5mg
- Carbs: 54g

Raspberry Compote

Preparation Time: 11 minutes

Cooking Time: 30 minutes

Servings: 2

Ingredients:

- 1 cup raspberries
- ½ cup Swerve
- 1 tsp freshly grated lemon zest

1 tsp vanilla extract

2 cups water

Directions:

1. Press the SAUTÉ button on your Instant Pot, then add all the listed Ingredients.

2. Stir well and pour in 1 cup of water.

3. Cook for 5 minutes, continually stirring, then pour in 1 more cup of water and press the CANCEL button.

4. Secure the lid properly, press the MANUAL button, and set the timer to 15 minutes on LOW pressure.

5. When the timer buzzes, press the CANCEL button and release the pressure naturally for 10 minutes.

6. Move the pressure handle to the "venting" position to release any remaining pressure and open the lid.

7. Let it cool before serving.

Nutrition:

Calories: 48

Fat: 0.5g

Carbs: 5g

Protein: 1g

Lemon Curd

Preparation Time: 10 minutes

Cooking Time: 10 minutes

Servings: 2

Ingredients:

4 tbsp. butter

1 cup sugar

2/3 cup lemon juice

3 eggs

2 tsp. lemon zest

1 ½ cups of water

Directions:

1. Whisk the butter and sugar thoroughly until smooth.

2. Add 2 whole eggs and incorporate just the yolk of the other egg.

3. Add the lemon juice.

4. Transfer the mixture into the two jars and tightly seal the tops

5. Pour 1 ½ cups of water into the bottom of the Instant Pot and place in steaming rack. Put the jars on the rack and cook on HIGH PRESSURE for 10 minutes.

6. Natural-release the pressure for 10 minutes before quick releasing the rest.

7. Stir in the zest and put the lids back on the jars.

Nutrition:

- Calories: 45
- Fat: 1g
- Carbs: 8g
- Protein: 1g

Sweet Chai Bites

Preparation Time: 20 minutes

Cooking Time: 45 minutes

Servings: 6

Ingredients:

- 1 cup cream cheese
- 1 cup coconut oil
- 2 ounces butter, grass-fed
- 2 teaspoons ginger
- 2 teaspoons cardamom
- 1 teaspoon nutmeg
- 1 teaspoon cloves
- 1 teaspoon vanilla extract, pure
- 1 teaspoon Darjeeling black tea
- Stevia to taste

Directions:

1. Melt your coconut oil and butter before adding in your black tea. Allow it to set for one to two minutes.

2. Add in your cream cheese, removing your mixture from heat.

3. Add in all of your spices, and stir to combine.

4. Pour into molds, and freeze before serving.

Nutrition:

- Calories: 178
- Protein: 1g
- Fat: 19g

Mozzarella Sticks

Preparation Time: 8 minutes

Cooking Time: 2 minutes

Servings: 2

Ingredients:

- 1 large whole egg
- 3 sticks mozzarella cheese in half (frozen overnight)
- 2 tablespoon grated parmesan cheese
- 1/2 cup almond flour
- 1/4 cup coconut oil
- 2 1/2 teaspoons Italian seasoning blend
- 1 tablespoon chopped parsley

- 1/2 teaspoon salt

Directions:

1.   Heat the coconut oil in a cast-iron skillet of medium size over low-medium heat.

2.   Crack the egg in a small bowl in the meantime and beat it well.

3.   Take another bowl of medium size and add parmesan cheese, almond flour, and seasonings to it. Whisk together the ingredients until a smooth mixture is prepared.

4.   Take the overnight frozen mozzarella stick and dip in the beaten egg, then coat it well with the dry mixture. Do the same with all the remaining cheese sticks.

5.   Place all the coated sticks in the preheated skillet and cook them for 2 minutes or until they start giving a golden-brown look from all sides.

6.   Remove from the skillet once cooked properly and place over a paper towel so that any extra oil gets absorbed.

7.   Sprinkle parsley over the sticks if you desire and serve with keto marinara sauce.

Nutrition:

- Calories: 430
- Fat: 39g
- Carbohydrates: 10g
- Protein: 20g

Braised Apples

Preparation Time: 5 minutes
Cooking Time: 12 minutes
Servings: 2
Ingredients:

- 2 cored apples
- ½ cup of water
- ½ cup red wine
- 3 tbsp. sugar
- ½ tsp. ground cinnamon

Directions:

1.   In the bottom of Instant Pot, add the water and place apples.

2.   Pour wine on top and sprinkle with sugar and cinnamon. Close the lid carefully and cook for 10 minutes at HIGH PRESSURE.

3.   When done, do a quick pressure release.

4.   Transfer the apples onto serving plates and top with cooking liquid.

5.   Serve immediately.

Nutrition:

- Calories: 245
- Fat: 0.5g
- Carbs: 53g

- Protein: 1g

Yogurt Mint

Preparation Time: 5 minutes
Cooking Time: 10 minutes
Servings: 2
Ingredients:

- 1 cup of water
- 5 cups of milk
- ¾ cup plain yogurt
- ¼ cup fresh mint
- 1 tbsp. maple syrup

Directions:

1.   Add 1 cup water to the Instant Pot Pressure Cooker.

2.   Press the STEAM function button and adjust to 1 minute.

3.   Once done, add the milk, then press the YOGURT function button and allow boiling.

4.   Add yogurt and fresh mint, then stir well.

5.   Pour into a glass and add maple syrup.

6.   Enjoy.

Nutrition:

- Calories: 25
- Fat: 0.5g
- Carbs: 5g
- Protein: 2g

Cinnamon Bites

Preparation Time: 20 minutes
Cooking Time: 95 minutes
Servings: 6
Ingredients:

- 1/8 teaspoon nutmeg
- 1 teaspoon vanilla extract
- ¼ teaspoon cinnamon
- 4 tablespoons coconut oil
- ½ cup butter, grass-fed
- 8 ounces cream cheese
- Stevia to taste

Directions:

1.   Soften your coconut oil and butter, mixing in your cream cheese.

2.   Add all of your remaining ingredients, and mix well.

3.   Pour into molds, and freeze until set.

Nutrition:

- Calories: 178
- Protein: 1g
- Fat: 19g

Conclusion

Anyone who's tried should understand that discovering the best diet of any kind can be somewhat of a challenge. The fact that there are seemly infinite ways to help you lose weight by strict diets, weight loss pills, programs, fads, gimmicks, and everything in between, can all-too-easily be overwhelming. But scientific studies and results on common people show that the Lean and Green diet is the best choice you can make.

The gist of the book is that to lose weight, you have to be on a meal plan. You follow the menu found on the packaging, and you cannot deviate from the route.

Under the Lean and Green diet, you're instructed to cut calories, not use medications. You're not going to lose thirty pounds in a week. You're not going to find it under the sofa or in the back of your closet. If you're following the chart, there won't be any leftovers.

The diet is carefully targeted at recording the calories you take in, as well as the calories you expel. The program is clear cut, so you know exactly what you're going to eat, and you know exactly what it's going to cost. There are no surprises, you can use your mobile phone to check your app, and you can look at the shopping list on the website.

www.ingramcontent.com/pod-product-compliance
Lightning Source LLC
Chambersburg PA
CBHW080307030726
47593CB00009B/2666